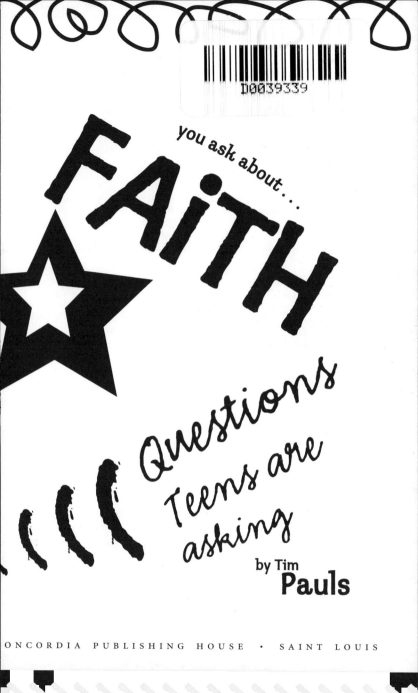

you ask about...

FAiTH

Questions
Teens are
asking

by Tim
Pauls

ONCORDIA PUBLISHING HOUSE · SAINT LOUIS

Library of Congress Cataloging-in-Publication Data

Pauls, Tim, 1967-
  You ask about faith : questions teens are asking / by Tim Pauls.
    p. cm.
  ISBN 978-0-7586-1493-3
  1. Christianity--Miscellanea. 2. Theology--Miscellanea. I. Title.

  BR121.3.P38 2008
  234'.23--dc22

                                                2008004763

1 2 3 4 5 6 7 8 9 10   17 16 15 14 13 12 11 10 09 08

For my parents, Gerald and Anna Pauls, who brought their children to the baptismal font at the earliest of ages so we might be given faith, and then hauled us to church pert-near every Sunday so we could hear the faith and grow in faith. You're God's instruments. Thank you.

Thanks to:

Pastor Mike McCoy, who once again donated a lot of time to proof this book and carefully answer my oft-scatterbrained e-mails. There are many helpful tweaks to the text for which he is responsible and I am grateful.

Pastor David Hrachovina, my colleague at Good Shepherd Lutheran Church, who has taught me much about the faith, living by faith, and clinging to the cross.

My bride, Teresa, with whom I spent many a night this past summer on the back patio discussing the Christian faith while this book was undertaken. Let's do so again soon.

My boys, Nathan and Noah, whom God has gifted with a living faith and lively intellects that want to talk about Jesus.

Table of Contents

Two Things to Get Started

8

Before we get into the body of this book, there are two things we have to get straight.

1. This Book is about both Faith and the Faith

When we talk about *faith*, we're going to use the term to refer to two different things. I'm not making up a new definition: if you check any dictionary, you'll find that *faith* has more than one meaning.

For one thing, *faith* can mean trust, belief,

confidence, and so forth—as in "I have faith in God." In this case, *faith* is trust. It's sometimes called "personal faith."

On the other hand, *faith* can also refer to a religion or a body of beliefs, as in "I am part of the Christian faith," or "the Holy Spirit . . . keeps us in the one true faith." In that case, *faith* is what you trust in.

The Bible uses *faith* both ways:

> * Faith as trust: "For we walk by faith, not by sight" **(2 Corinthians 5:7)**.

> * Faith as what you trust in: "Be watchful, stand firm in the faith, act like men, be strong" **(1 Corinthians 16:13)**.

9

Therefore, as Christians, we have faith in the faith: we believe what God says.

If you're into Latin—which seems to be making a comeback these days—or you just want to impress your pastor next Sunday, these are often discussed with the following terms: faith which believes is called *fides qua creditur*. Add an "e" to your "qua" (which is legal in most states) and you get *fides quae creditur*, which is the phrase for the faith which you believe. Neither of these is *fides quack creditor*, which sounds like it means, "You'd better believe you owe the duck money." I don't think it means that, though. Alas, I digress.

In any given Bible text, how can you tell which one the Bible is talking about? Sometimes, the grammar helps: *the faith* will mean "what you believe in." A lot of the time, it's context. Sometimes, it may not be completely clear—because *faith* and *the faith* go together. Without the faith, you have nothing to have faith in. Without faith, you can't believe the faith. Get it? (Just in case you didn't, what I meant to say was that without the Word of God, you have nothing to believe in; and without faith, you can't believe the Word of God.) We'll take a look at some of these Scripture passages along the way.

For now, I just want to make sure you're in tune with the idea that *faith* will refer to two different—yet very-much connected—things in this book, just as it does in the Bible.

Which brings us to the second important point of this little introduction.

2. God's Word is the Source of Christian Faith

If you want to know about Christian doctrine, the Bible is the source. It's God's Word. Sure, it was written down by men, but it's still God's Word. It's without error, so it's the final authority.

We really can't take this for granted. For one thing, a lot of people—even many who call themselves Christians—believe that the Bible isn't God's Word. They may believe it's man's word about God, or partly God's Word and partly man's opinion, or a very nice "book of wisdom" like the Qur'an or the sayings of Confucius. We're going to give the Bible the credit it deserves—it's God's Word. It's the final Word on all that we believe.

For another thing, many people believe that the Bible is just one source of Christian teaching among many. They would say that, along with the Bible, God might reveal new messages through dreams, prophets, feelings, events, or new additions to the Bible today. Again, we're going to go with what the Bible says as the final authority.

How to Interpret the Bible: Let God's Word Speak for Itself!

Even then, we have to say more. All sorts of people use the Bible to say whatever they want it to say—even to contradict Christianity. They might do this by using a verse or two out of context or asserting that the Bible has changed in meaning over time. Therefore, we have to take a moment and make clear how we're going to treat the Bible. We can boil this down into three easy steps:

First, we're going to base our teaching on clear passages of Scripture. Some portions of Scripture make more sense to us than others. For instance, "Thou shalt not steal" means "Don't take what belongs to your neighbor." It does not mean "Pizza is good breakfast food." The meaning is clear to us: that's why we can teach the Seventh Commandment with confidence. Thus we get to rule number one of interpreting the Bible: *we base our teachings on the clear passages of Scripture.*

12

But what if a text isn't so clear to us? Do we make something up and say, "Thus says the Lord"? No. Let's say that you read something in this book that doesn't make sense to you. Who's the best person to ask what I meant? Me! (And with Google and all these days, that's pretty easy to do.) You can ask a friend or a stranger or your dog, but I should likely have a better idea of what I'm thinking than they do. So who should we ask if something in God's Word doesn't make sense? God, of course! Where does He speak to us? In the Bible! Therefore, when we don't understand what a part of the Bible is saying, we look to the rest of the Bible to see if there are other passages to help us out.

For example, in Revelation 5:6, John writes, "I saw a Lamb standing, as though it had been slain, with seven horns and with seven eyes, which are the seven spirits of God sent out into all the earth." On its own, the meaning of this verse isn't exactly clear. You, being the diligent student of the Scriptures and generally sharp cookie that you are, say, "This means that Mom should let me go to that party with my buddies on Friday!" No, wait. That's what you don't say, because you're not going to twist the Bible to fit what you want. Instead, you're going to say, "I'll use Scripture to decode this. Back in Exodus 12, the Passover lamb was slain and its blood spread on the doors so those inside remained alive. This pointed to Jesus, whom John the Baptist called "the Lamb of God, who takes away the sin of the world" (John 1:29). Therefore, the Lamb in Revelation—who had been slain but is now alive—is Jesus, who was crucified for my sins and raised on the third day." Furthermore, you do a little study and say, "I can't find 'seven spirits of God' anywhere in the Bible; but back in Isaiah 11:2, the Holy Spirit is described with seven different attributes, so the 'seven spirits of God' here are really the Holy Spirit." Thus you've used the rest of the Bible to determine what a puzzling passage means. And you've brought us (good

13

job!) to rule number two of interpreting the Bible: *when a passage is unclear to us, we look to the rest of the Bible to explain it.*

Sometimes, though, we still can't find a satisfactory answer. A good example would be 1 Corinthians 15:29: "Otherwise, what do people mean by being baptized on behalf of the dead? If the dead are not raised at all, why are people baptized on their behalf?" What does it mean to be "baptized on behalf of the dead"? Many have searched the Scriptures, researched the history of Corinth at the time, and done all sorts of other studies; but the definite meaning of this verse eludes us. It was clear to the Christians at Corinth then, but it sure isn't to us now. Scholars have offered suggestions—hundreds of them. But we can't say for sure what this verse means. This brings us to rule number three of interpreting the Bible: *when we don't know what a passage means, we say we don't know.* We don't require people to believe what isn't certain. We can offer opinions and educated guesses about it, but we'd better make clear that we're not sure. This seems pretty clear: if you don't know what I'm saying, I don't want you making stuff up and putting words in my mouth—and we should be far more concerned about making stuff up about the Bible and putting words in God's mouth that He didn't say.

Yet, too often, people have claimed they know the meaning of a passage because of some feeling or dream or other inspiration, or because it conveniently fits what they want. We're not going to operate that way. Instead, we're going to stick with God's Word in the Bible. That's where we're sure that God speaks.

So, one more time, the three rules for interpreting the Bible:

1. We base what we teach on clear passages.

2. If a passage is unclear to us, we look to the rest of the Bible to explain it.

3. Where we still don't know what a passage means, we admit we don't know.

If you've got those three rules down, we're ready to learn about *faith* and *the faith*—both of which come to us from God in His Word. We'll answer a few questions here, and then get started.

—Tim Pauls

Q&A:
You Ask . . .

16

How do we know that the Bible really is God's Word?

The answer sounds strange at first, but here it is: the Bible says so with verses like 2 Timothy 3:16, "All Scripture is breathed out by God and profitable for teaching, for reproof, for correction, and for training in righteousness." In other words, the Bible is self-authenticating: it's God's Word because it says so, and we believe it.

The first reaction often is, "That's no proof. In this world, self-authentication doesn't work. We need proof and witnesses. I mean, if I say I'm Spider-Man, you're not going to believe me." At this point, I try to be helpful by saying something like, "Of course not, because we can't both be Spider-Man." Actually, a more helpful response is this: it's true that in this world, we want additional proof. When I write a check at a store, I need to show some ID to prove who I am. I can't vouch for me. But here's the thing: whether or not I show the ID—and whether or not people believe me, I am Tim Pauls. My identity doesn't depend on who people think I am. Thanks be to God for that!

You and I are conditioned to demand proof. We want proof that people are who they claim to be, because people are sinful and often lie. We want proof because we're used to courtroom scenes where guilt must be established by evidence beyond reasonable doubt. And we want proof because we live in a very scientific world, where things must be proven repeatedly in order to be accepted as true. (Well, except for evolution, which usually gets a free pass, a bouquet of flowers, and a weekend trip to a spa just for being so ridiculous.) But God isn't a liar, a criminal, or a science project. He's God, and we shouldn't try to submit Him to our tests for things of this world. (We talked about this quite a bit in the first book of this series, *You Ask about Life*, so I won't go into much more detail here.) Instead, we take God at His

Word, and He says that the Bible is His Word. We don't agree just because we've proven it, or because God has shown us two pieces of ID and an envelope with His home address on it. We believe this to be true by faith—the faith that God gives in His Word—which, happily, is what the rest of this book is about.

My friend said we should be able to understand everything in the Bible, because God wouldn't have given us a book we couldn't understand. What do you think?

18

I've heard this before. Among others, Jehovah's Witnesses teach this, saying that God would be unkind if He gave us a book we couldn't understand—and no one wants God to be unkind.

However, there are a few problems with this. First, what does it say about God? Nowhere in the Bible does it promise that we'll be able to understand all of Scripture. If we say God is unkind when we can't understand something, we're saying things about God that He doesn't say about Himself. We're putting words in His mouth. I think a similar argument would be, "Why would God give us Law that we couldn't keep? Isn't that unkind?" Answer: God's Law doesn't make Him unkind; it shows Him to be holy and us to be sinful.

Second, the question must be asked: if the entire Bible is guaranteed to be understood, then by whom? Three-year-olds can't understand all of it—so is God unkind to three-year-olds? Is the Bible only for adults? Ah, but not all adults have the same intellect, so not all of them will understand all of Scripture—so is God unkind to people with lower IQs? Exactly who can understand all of the Bible?

I foresee the real danger of this argument: it makes sense that if all of the Bible can be understood (and I'm not saying that it can), then there will only be a few who can understand it because the rest of us are too young or dumb. If that's true, then those few need to say to the rest of us, "Since you can't understand all of Scripture, and we do, you'll have to let us tell you what it means and abide by what we say." See? This argument sets up a situation where only a select few can really explain the Bible—and those select few can then go on to twist what it says with the excuse that only they know what it really means, and we just don't understand.

Look, it's just plain silly for anyone to claim to fully understand the Bible. As we already said, the Bible makes no such promise—so to say this is to make a rule about the Bible that God hasn't made. We also have tiny, sinful, finite minds and different levels of intellect. Furthermore, we're limited by history—a lot of the customs that took place in the Bible are shrouded by time. It would certainly be presumptuous to guarantee that we can understand all that God says in Scripture.

Here's a better teaching. On the one hand, we rejoice that God is bigger and wiser than we are, and we confess we're not as big and wise and holy as He is. That's what St. Paul says:

> Oh, the depth of the riches and wisdom and knowledge of God! How unsearchable are His judgments and how inscrutable His ways! "For who has known the mind of the Lord, or who has been His counselor?"
> **(Romans 11:33–34)**

On the other hand, we give thanks for this: we're not saved by knowing everything. We're saved because Jesus died for us, and God makes that perfectly clear in the Bible. While we can never fully comprehend the Scriptures, they do make us wise unto salvation (2 Timothy 3:15) because they tell us about Jesus and give us faith. That's what we need for now: we'll know a lot more in heaven (1 Corinthians 13:12).

if we don't understand the Bible, does that mean God is unclear?

No. God is perfect and perfectly clear. It's our sinful, tiny minds that cloud and fail to comprehend His Word.

You've limited us to hearing from God only through His Word—through the Bible. Why can't God speak through dreams or visions today? What about someone who has said he's had a new revelation from God?

I'm glad you said I've limited *us*—not that I've limited God from speaking in other ways. The truth is God can do whatever He wants. However, we can be absolutely certain that He speaks to us in the Bible, because we know it's His Word. At the beginning of Hebrews, we read, "Long ago, at many times and in many ways, God spoke to our fathers by the prophets, but in these last days He has spoken to us by His Son . . ." (Hebrews 1:1–2). In the Old Testament, the Lord used all sorts of visions, events, signs, and wonders to reveal His plans and point to Jesus. But now that Jesus has come, we listen to Him. Where does Jesus speak? He speaks to us in His Word: "These are written so that you may believe that Jesus is the Christ, the Son of God, and that by believing you may have life in His name" (John 20:31). When we hear Him speak in Scripture, we know it's Jesus who's talking to us.

So let's say that somebody or some group claims to have a new revelation from Jesus—how do you know it's true? You have to test the message:

> Beloved, do not believe every spirit, but test the spirits to see whether they are from God, for many false prophets have gone out into the world. By this you know the Spirit of God: every spirit that confesses that Jesus Christ has come in the flesh is from God, and every spirit that does not confess Jesus is not from God. **(1 John 4:1–3)**

So how do you know the message truly confesses Jesus—how do you know it says the same thing Jesus says? Because it agrees with the Bible—that's your standard.

> * If someone's message contradicts the Bible, then it's not from the Lord.
>
> * If it agrees with the Bible, then that's where he got it from in the first place and it isn't a new revelation.
>
> * If it does neither, then how could

you ask about . . . FAiTH

you ever be sure that it really was from God, and not from somebody's imagination?

One more thought: let's say someone is sincerely convinced he's seen God in a vision. Is this absolutely, completely impossible? No! Again, God can do whatever He wants. But how can you be sure it wasn't just a vivid dream concocted in the dark recesses of this person's mind? How can you be sure it was God? You can't. On the other hand, God's Word is sure.

Stick with the Bible as your source of God's Word to you. Whenever anyone tells you what God says—including your pastor—test it against the Bible. When you hear it there, you're sure it's God doing the talking; and it's there that He tells you all you need to know about His plans for you.

23

You used 1 Corinthians 15:29 as an example of a verse we don't understand. Based on that verse, Mormons baptize people on behalf of the dead: Are they right? Do they understand something we don't?

This is actually a good example of the previous question, where someone has had a "new revelation" that supposedly came from the Lord. Imagine someone saying, "Last night, God told me what 1 Corinthians 15:29 really means. And since I say it's God who told me, it must be true!" Would you believe him? You shouldn't.

Mormons cite 1 Corinthians 15:29 as a basis for baptizing the dead, in order to help the dead earn their salvation. However, they explain this Bible passage by means of another book, *The Doctrine and Covenants of the Church of Jesus Christ of Latter-day Saints*. For example, D&C 127:5–9 specifies how these baptisms are to be recorded. *Doctrine and Covenants* is a collection of writings by Joseph Smith, the founder of Mormonism; and Smith declares that these are revelations from God. In this case, he's the one saying, "I have a new revelation from God, so you have to believe what I say."

Do you? No! I have friends who belong to the LDS (Latter-day Saints) church, but I can't agree with what they teach. In this case, we know this teaching about baptism for the dead is wrong, because the Bible makes clear that we can't earn salvation (see section 1), and that there is no possibility for one to be converted after death: "It is appointed for man to die once, and after that comes judgment" (Hebrews 9:27). Whatever 1 Corinthians 15:29 means, it doesn't

24

mean what the Mormon Church teaches.

I've heard stories about tornadoes that wiped out the bars but left the churches intact. People say that's proof of God at work. What do you think?

If that's true, what was God trying to prove—that the town needed remodeled bars, while it could keep the old church buildings? Or if that's true, then what about the one where the tornado takes out the churches and leaves the bars? Tornadoes aren't exactly discriminating, and a lot of church buildings have been demolished that way.

25

Here's the point: don't try to discern God's will from what you see in nature. When people do this, they're using some event to tell you what they think God is saying. You're going to see some beautiful sunsets and some terrible storms. Everybody does, whether they're Christians or not. If you want to hear what God says to you, stick to His Word.

Does God speak through feelings?

By *feelings*, I suppose you could mean emotions or instincts. Let's talk quickly about both.

Emotions are a gift from God: He's created you to have feelings. However, like everything else, they can lead you astray if you let them take the place of God and His Word. A lot of people say, to paraphrase an old song, "Something can't be wrong if it feels so right." So they go on to commit whatever sin they want because their feelings must be a better source of God's Word than the Bible. Look, sometimes you're going to feel mad and want to bite somebody's head off (not literally, I hope); that doesn't mean it's okay to do so, but probably that you need to repent of your anger. You might feel tempted to sexual immorality—and a lot of people defend sexual sin by saying it feels so good. I think the point is clear: don't rely on your feelings to know what God wants; hear Him speak to you in His Word.

Along with emotions, you have instincts, "gut feelings" that are commonly associated with common sense: "I have a feeling that I shouldn't trust that stranger who wants me to give him my wallet and house key." Common sense is a gift of God too; and I'd argue that you have these instincts because God has put His Law into your heart so you know not to trust people who haven't proven trustworthy. Another example might be, "Harold had a funny feeling, so he took the train instead of the bus to work—and the bus was in an awful crash." In this instance, we give thanks that God has preserved Harold's safety. At the same time, though, was God sending a specific message to Harold? No, not that any of us can ever know for sure. If anything, such mercies are given to draw us to hear what God says in the Bible about the mercy of forgiveness in Jesus.

What if i really feel in my heart that God is telling me something?

Make certain it agrees with the Bible. Speaking of which, the Lord declares, "The heart is deceitful above all things, and desperately sick; who can understand it?" (Jeremiah 17:9). Your heart is part of you; you're sinful and you can easily deceive yourself. Therefore, never trust a feeling that contradicts God's Word.

What about faith and science? Do they oppose each other?

I wrote about this quite a bit in the first book of this series, *You Ask about Life*, so I won't repeat myself here. Briefly, though, here's the deal: science and faith are not opposed to each other. However, they do cover different realms. Science is all about studying the natural world God has created: astronomy and physics and medicine and the aerodynamics of flying spoons and more. Faith is about trusting in Jesus and the forgiveness He's won by His death and resurrection. Don't mix up the two. Just because you can't prove scientifically that Jesus rose from the dead doesn't mean it didn't happen. The faith says that He has. Likewise, don't just believe that your car's brakes are going to work. They're part of this natural world—test them out before you roll downhill.

Can people be Christians but not believe in Jesus?

The answer is simple, once you get the definitions down, but people keep redefining what *Christian* means. For instance, some say Christians are those who try to live by the Ten Commandments; but a lot of non-Christians believe murder and theft are wrong, so that's hardly a unique mark. Others boil it down to helping those in need: Christians should indeed help those in need, but this is also something lots of non-Christians do. Some will say they're Christians because they believe in Jesus, but they don't believe He was anything more than a nice guy. Mormons and Jehovah's Witnesses both claim to be true Christians—even as their theology explicitly condemns Christianity! Others define it by the family tree: Christians are those who have descended from people who lived in a country once ruled by the Church. (For instance, the Swedish population is over 90 percent Lutheran because a ruler said so in the past—but only a few actually go to church.) Still others define *Christian* as "acting in a loving manner and giving people what they desire." In that case, you have "Christians" campaigning for things the Bible condemns, such as abortion or gay marriage. You can't reconcile that with Jesus, who said, "If you love Me, you will keep My commandments" (John 14:15).

All of this is to say: if you ask around, a lot of people will say they're Christians, even if they don't believe in Jesus.

So what does *Christian* mean? Here's a crazy idea: let's let the Bible define *Christian* for us! In Acts 11:26, we read, "In Antioch the disciples were first called Christians." Why? Because they were nice people? Because they were Swedish? No, because they'd spent a year listening to Paul teach them all about Jesus, and they believed in Him. Please note that it wasn't an especially popular thing to say, "I

29

follow Jesus, whom the Romans condemned and crucified, and I believe He's risen from the dead." But trusting in Jesus, they were willing to bear His name. Likewise, in Acts 26, Paul stood before King Agrippa on trial and made a defense of his faith. He declared that Jesus had suffered, died, and risen from the dead. After this, Agrippa said, "In a short time would you persuade me to be a Christian?" (Acts 26:28). In other words, faith in Jesus and His work was what made someone a Christian. It still is today.

Now that we've got the definitions down—414 words later—the answer is easy: no! You can't be a Christian without believing in Jesus, the Son of God, who died for your sins and rose again from the dead.

A lot of my friends believe in the Rapture. is it safe to say that a biblical teaching must be true if a lot of Christians believe it?

No. It's possible that the majority of Christians can get a biblical teaching wrong. The truth of God's Word isn't determined by majority vote, no matter how sincere the voters. The truth of God's Word is determined by

God's Word, which is why we follow those three rules I outlined above.

The Rapture is a great example. A lot of Christians—especially in America—believe that one day, before the end of the world, all Christians will suddenly disappear from the earth while the world continues for a while. This isn't going to happen. Those who teach the Rapture cite several verses that sound convincing at first, but their method violates the three rules above. Likewise, a lot of Christians today deny that God gives forgiveness to infants in Holy Baptism, but that doesn't mean they're right. We'll talk a lot more about that one later, but first we need to lay the groundwork by talking about faith.

Section One: The Faith

As we've already seen, *faith* and *the faith* are inseparably connected for Christians. In fact, before we can really take a look at what *faith* is there are some parts of *the faith* we need to make absolutely clear. That's what this chapter is about. This isn't meant to be a comprehensive look at the Christian faith—that would take far too much space and time, and I'm assuming this is a review for you. Rather, I present to you the following points because I'm making this argument: *faith* and *the faith* are so inseparable that your understanding of salvation will directly affect your understanding of what faith is. We'll start with you . . .

You

1. You're sinful.

That isn't a very good start for you at all, but the Bible makes clear this is the case: "Therefore, just as sin came into the world through one man, and death through sin, and so death spread to all men because all sinned" (Romans 5:12). Like everyone else, you're sinful from birth—actually, from the moment you were conceived. "Behold, I was brought forth in iniquity, and in sin did my mother conceive me" (Psalm 51:5).

33

Now, just to be clear, we want to make a distinction between *original* sin and *actual* sin. Most people think of *sin* as the things that they say, think, and do that are wrong. Those are examples of *actual* sin, but they're not the big problem. Don't get me wrong, they're enough of a problem to condemn you, but the worse trouble would be *original* sin.

Let's say, for example, that you have the flu—there's a nasty influenza virus coursing through your bloodstream, making you feel wretched. In fact, you've got the clogged sinuses, the hacking cough, the upset stomach, the fever, the achy joints, and everything that goes with the flu. At this point, on advice from your doctor, you take some medicine to help with all the misery. It's amazing stuff. In fact, you don't feel congested or nauseous or achy or feverish. You feel great! You feel like going outside and playing croquet with Spam!

Quiz time: At this point, are you healthy?

Answer: No. You've managed to knock down the symptoms; but as long as that flu virus is still inside you, you're still sick. The virus—not its symptoms—is the bigger problem. In fact, some people serve as "carriers" for diseases; they never feel the symptoms themselves, but they carry a virus inside and spread it to others.

Original sin is like the virus: the actual sins you think and say and do are sins, yes, but they're not the big problem. The big problem is that you're born sinful through and through on the inside; and as long as you're sinful, you're going to do sinful things.

The answer, of course, is to get rid of your sin. But how?

In the New Testament, the Pharisees had a plan for this: they figured that as long as they cleaned up their act and stopped sinning on the outside, they must be clean and sinless on the inside too. In other words, as long as they got rid of their actual sins, they thought they'd be good to go for God. In their quest for holiness, they made up a bunch of strict rules and did their best to live by them. How successful were they? They fooled themselves and thought they were doing a great job, but all they'd managed to do was knock down some of the symptoms of the real problem. They'd cut down somewhat on actual sins of word and deed, but they couldn't do anything about their original sin inside. This led Jesus to call them "whitewashed tombs" (Matthew 23:27). They looked very nice on the outside, like a tomb with a fresh coat of paint. But inside, they were dead in their sin and couldn't do anything to get rid of their sin.

35

This brings us to something else about you, something you share with the Pharisees and everybody else.

2. You're dead.

It's not the sort of thing you want to hear, but I present to you Ephesians 2:1–2:

> And you were dead in the trespasses
> and sins in which you once walked,
> following the course of this world, fol-

> lowing the prince of the power of the
> air, the spirit that is now at work in
> the sons of disobedience.

According to the Bible, you're born dead in your trespasses and sins. Your body is alive, sure—your heart is beating and you might be able to do math problems and make funny noises with your armpits—but your soul has no life. It's cut off from God because of your sin.

Now if you spend your time watching television instead of reading fine books like this one, you've probably seen a medical drama now and then. I've seen a bunch of them; and at least once per hour, there's some poor dude in the ER whose heart has stopped beating. There's a flat line on the monitor. He's dead, and he's going to be deader in a few more minutes unless something is done.

(By the way, we'll be referring to this guy several times throughout the book, so we need to give him a name. Being the imaginative, creative thinker that I am, we'll call him "Deadguy.")

So anyway, Deadguy isn't doing very well, and you know what has to be done. "Defibulize him!" you're thinking. Something like that, anyway. "Get those little paddles out, put some goo on them, yell 'clear!' and then shock him back to life!" You're right—that's what they usually do. But here's what they never do: in all my time watching medical dramas, not once—not even one time!—have the doctors put the paddles in the patient's hands and said, "Sir, if you'll just shock yourself now, it's all going to be okay." Think about that: the show's story line might include a toddler who is half-boy/half-toaster and a woman cooking pancakes for extra-terrestrials; but the writers have never done something so unbelievable as the doctors handing the paddles to Deadguy.

Why have they never done this? Because the poor guy is dead. He can't help himself. If he's going to be alive again, somebody else is going to have to save him. Dead people can't make themselves alive.

37

Before God, you're dead in sin. Apart from Jesus, you're Deadguy. (Or Deadgirl, but I don't want to write "Deadguy or Deadgirl" every time I just want to refer to the dude in the ER, even if that would boost my word count for the editors just like this long, relatively useless sentence is doing; so I'll count on you to have the smarts to understand that *Deadguy* can refer to either men or women.) You can't save yourself, even if you're half toaster. That means somebody else has to save you.

But wait! There's more to your plight.

3. You're also blind.

This makes sense, you being dead and all. But here's what the Bible says. "The natural person does not accept the things of the Spirit of God, for they are folly to him, and he is not able to understand them because they are spiritually discerned" (1 Corinthians 2:14). Thanks to sin, God's Word sounds foolish. As Christians, we easily declare that Jesus died on the cross to take away our sins; but without God working in us, that sounds completely ridiculous. If you'd like, take a newspaper and go out to a field full of cows. Locate the cow closest to the fence and start telling it the day's headlines. Read a story or two, and watch the cow's reaction. You will note the cow staring at you intently, chewing its cud; and you will also be aware that the cow has no idea what you're doing or what you're saying. All it hears is "blah-blah-blah." Frankly, it finds the grass it's chewing far more fascinating than you.

(You will also note the farmer staring at you in quite a different manner than the cow, wondering if you're dangerous or just a little bit off. But that's a topic for a different book, *You Ask about Conversations with Farm Animals*.)

You and I are the cows when it comes to God's Word. Without His work, the Gospel just doesn't make sense. Actually, we're in worse shape than the cows. For one thing, as previously mentioned, we're dead. For another, it's not just because we have a low intellect and need to be all learnified. It's not a matter of ignorance, it's a matter of unbelief. As long as we're dead in sin, we cannot believe God's Word.

For this blindness, it's not a matter of just putting on a good pair of glasses—that doesn't help dead cows see. No, to see, we need to be made alive. Which brings us back to the big problem. We can't give life to ourselves. Somebody else has to make us alive, make us see.

Anyway, I'm sure you have few greater pleasures in life than reading a book that calls you a dead cow. We can't dwell on that forever, though. We must move on to the next truth about you—namely, that you're not just dead and blind in sin.

4. You're also an enemy of God.

Don't take my word for it. Take *the Word* for it, like Genesis 8:21: "The intention of man's heart is evil from his youth." Furthermore, "For the mind that is set on the flesh is hostile to God, for it does not submit to God's law; indeed, it cannot" (Romans 8:7). According to the Bible,

39

you start out an enemy of God. Sounds harsh, doesn't it? Almost unbelievable? But think this through: God commands, "You shall love the Lord your God with all your heart and with all your soul and with all your mind and with all your strength" (Mark 12:30). Anything less than that is sinful and unholy, which makes you sinful and unholy. That makes you an enemy of God.

Let's look at another verse that's probably familiar to you:

> I the LORD your God am a jealous God,
> visiting the iniquity of the fathers
> on the children to the third and the
> fourth generation of those who hate
> Me, but showing steadfast love to
> thousands of those who love Me and
> keep My commandments.
> **(Exodus 20:5–6)**

The Lord declares that those who love Him are those who keep His commandments (see also John 14:15). Those who don't keep His commandments hate Him—they are His enemies. Therefore, if we sin, we're enemies of God.

This is a difficult one to accept, I think, because hatred and enmity (being an enemy) usually mean an intense feeling of dislike. A few people devote their lives to proving that

God doesn't exist or isn't very nice, but not very many have such obvious dedication as enemies of God. A lot of people don't voice anger at God, but they're very angry at His Word when He declares that practices such as abortion or premarital sex are sinful; and those who spend their time complaining about what Christians say are really complaining about Jesus (see Matthew 10:25). All in all, most people don't spend their days feeling an intense aversion for God. At least not yet. But consider this: if you've ever had an enemy, you don't spend every moment detesting him. You usually save those feelings until you see him or get a message from him; when he's not up in your grill, it's easy to ignore him. For now, that's what a lot of unbelievers do. Face-to-face with God on the Last Day, though, they'll realize their sin and hate His holiness.

By nature, you and I are enemies of God. Even now, we'll dislike His Word when He commands us not to do what we want to do. And when we oppose His Word, we oppose Him.

So there you go. You're dead in sin, blind in sin, and an enemy of God who is hostile to His Word. You're dead, you can't understand life, and you don't want to be alive. Furthermore, "the wages of sin is death" (Romans 6:23)—eternal death, separated in hell from God and His life.

At this point, two things should be clear:

First, you really, really need to be saved.

Second, you can't save yourself, what with being a dead, blind, enemy cow and all.

That should make a third thing very clear: if you're going to be saved, somebody else has to save you.

The Savior

Someone has saved you, namely Jesus. We could spend the rest of this book talking about who He is and what He's done, but we're going to hit some main points and leave it at that. If you find the next couple of paragraphs boring, I urge you to read the third question in this chapter's Q&A section and take it to heart.

1. Jesus is the Son of God.

God defines Himself as one God, but three persons—Father, Son, and Holy Spirit. This is called the Holy Trinity. All three persons are equally God, and all are all-knowing, all-powerful, all-present, and eternal. Jesus is the Son of God. He has been with the Father and the Holy Spirit from eternity. He's not a creation, He is God too (John 1:1, 10:30). As such, Jesus is all-knowing, all-powerful, all-present, and eternal.

Just to be as clear as we can, we want to avoid two ditches. One is the idea that we worship three different Gods. That's not true. God declares Himself to be one (Deuteronomy 6:4). The other is the idea that we worship one God who goes into three different modes; sometimes He's the Father, at other times He's the Son or the Spirit. That's not right either; several times in Scripture, God presents Himself as three different persons, like when Jesus was baptized (Luke 3:22). He's not one God wearing three hats. He's one God, but three distinct persons.

Still doesn't make sense? We do well to keep in mind that God is greater than our little minds. Since He says He's triune, His Word is good enough for us.

43

2. Jesus is fully God and fully man.

In keeping with His Father's will to save us, Jesus became flesh (John 1:14). He was miraculously conceived in the Virgin Mary by the Holy Spirit (Luke 1:35) and born a baby like you (Luke 2:7). Even today, He remains both fully God and fully man. We could list a bunch of passages here, but for now I'll direct you to Philippians 2:1–10.

This is a mystery beyond our understanding, just like the Trinity; so once again in order to clarify, we want to say what this doesn't mean.

This doesn't mean Jesus gave up being God in order to be man. It doesn't mean He only pretended to be human. It doesn't mean He was half-man and half-God. It doesn't mean God adopted Him when He was baptized and disinherited Him forever at the cross. All of these are teachings that have invaded the Church over the centuries, and all of them are wrong. Scripture says Jesus was one person, yet fully human and fully divine.

In fact, He still is one person, yet fully human and fully divine.

44

3. Jesus lived a perfect life.

Jesus didn't sin even once in thought, word, or deed (Hebrews 4:15). He kept God's Law perfectly. This has two great blessings for you. One is that He didn't have to die for His own sin, because He didn't have any. That means He could take your place and die for your sins (1 Peter 2:24). The other is that along with taking away your sins, He could give you the credit for His perfect life (2 Corinthians 5:21).

4. Jesus died on the cross.

Jesus was crucified for the sins of the world. Contrary to all sorts of loopy ideas put forth by the world, His death was no accident. It was God's plan for your salvation. However, even many Christians don't fully grasp what happened at the cross: God the Father condemned His Son for all the sins of all the world (Galatians 3:13). In other words, Jesus suffered hell on the cross. Afterward, He died and was laid in a tomb.

5. Jesus rose from the dead.

Three days later, He rose from the dead. He appeared to His disciples and to others several times (Acts 10:40–41), proving that He had conquered sin, death, and the power of the devil. He rose from the dead—body and all—to demonstrate that He's conquered the grave for you and He will raise you from the dead—body and all (1 Corinthians 15:51–57).

6. Jesus ascended into heaven.

He ascended into heaven (Acts 1:9–11) to sit at God's right hand (Romans 8:34) and work all things for your good—and to demonstrate that He would deliver you to heaven for eternity. At a time of the Father's choosing, Jesus will return to judge all people (2 Corinthians 5:10). Those who believe in Him will be delivered to heaven, but those who do not believe in Him will be condemned to hell.

By the way, it's probably worth noting that the first two points above are about who Jesus is, while the next four are about what Jesus has done. In other words, we've talked about His person and His work, and both are necessary for your salvation.

Free Salvation

Speaking of your salvation, here it is: Jesus has done it all. He's lived, died, risen, and ascended for you. By His suffering and death, He has made the sacrifice for your sin so God no longer holds your sin against you. In taking away your sin, He also has given you the credit for His perfect life: when God looks on you as one forgiven, He sees only Jesus' holiness and righteous works, because all your sins are gone. Jesus has risen from the dead to raise you from the dead, and He has ascended into heaven so you can ascend into heaven too.

He's done it all.

Now, as we've done before, we want to emphasize a few really important points.

1. Jesus has won salvation for all, not just for some.

Jesus didn't just die on the cross for some people. He didn't pick some ethnic groups and forsake others, nor did He favor men over women or adults over kids. Furthermore—and this is especially important—He didn't just die on the cross for believers. He died for all. We'll look at a couple of verses here, although there are more. John 3:16 makes this clear: "For God so loved the world, that He gave His only Son, that whoever believes in Him should not perish but have eternal life." So does 1 John 2:2: "He is the propitiation for our sins, and not for ours only but also for the sins of the whole world."

47

2. Jesus has won salvation for you.

You're not just a face in the crowd, unknown individually to God. Personally, I love this passage:

> Are not two sparrows sold for a
> penny? And not one of them will fall
> to the ground apart from your Father.
> But even the hairs of your head are all
> numbered. Fear not, therefore; you are
> of more value than many sparrows.
> **(Matthew 10:29–31)**

The Lord knows who you are by name. In fact, you can be absolutely sure that (and when and how) He gives forgiveness to you. More on that a little bit later on.

3. Salvation is absolutely free for you.

Time and time again, the Bible makes clear that salvation is a gift of God. Check out, for instance, Romans 3:22–24 ("For there is no distinction: for all have sinned and fall short of the glory of God, and are justified by His grace as a gift, through the redemption that is in Christ Jesus.") and Ephesians 2:8–9 ("For by grace you have been saved through faith. And this is not your own doing; it is the gift of God, not a result of works, so that no one may boast."). Both of these passages make clear that salvation is a gift. By definition, you don't have to pay for a gift. You don't have to work for a gift. If you have to pay for it or work for it, it's not a gift anymore.

You and I hear that often, but it's worth pondering for a couple of reasons.

For one, it's really quite astounding that the Lord gives salvation freely. When you're the only source of something that people want or people need, you can make them pay a lot.

Consider this: when the Wii came out, all sorts of people camped out at stores overnight to buy the first consoles. Some people bought five or six. Why? To give them away to underprivileged people? Hardly! They put them on eBay to sell for three times the price, and they made some pretty good money.

There's only one source for forgiveness and salvation: Jesus! It wasn't cheap for Him to acquire; He paid for your redemption with His own blood, with His innocent suffering and death. But He doesn't pass that cost on to you. He doesn't require you to do great things to get it. Instead, He gives it freely.

49

4. Jesus gives you more forgiveness than you could ever need.

I love this translation of Ephesians 1:7–8: "In Him we have redemption through His blood, the forgiveness of our trespasses, according to the riches of His grace, which He lavished upon us, in all wisdom and insight." Jesus lavishes the riches of His grace upon us. He doesn't give enough to cover a dozen sins a day, or send out a thirty-day trial supply. He gives you overflowing, abounding, more-than-you-need amounts of grace. When He forgives your sins,

He forgives all of them. "If we confess our sins, He is faithful and just to forgive us our sins and to cleanse us from all unrighteousness" (1 John 1:9).

5. With forgiveness, Jesus gives you every good gift from God.

If you're forgiven, you have God's favor and all good things.

> What then shall we say to these things? If God is for us, who can be against us? He who did not spare His own Son but gave Him up for us all, how will He not also with Him graciously give us all things?
> **(Romans 8:31–32)**

This includes eternal life: "Now if we have died with Christ, we believe that we will also live with Him" (Romans 6:8). It includes freedom from sin and God's strength to live by His Word: "He Himself bore our sins in His body on the tree, that we might die to sin and live to righteousness. By His wounds you have been healed" (1 Peter 2:24). In other words, you're not dead or blind or God's enemy anymore— and it's all because Jesus forgives all of your sins.

You're not a cow, either. But then again, that was only a metaphor in the first place.

A Big Difference

In every other religion in the world, people have to earn their salvation. Some teach that you have to do good works. Some teach that you have to convert the infidel or kill him. In the movies, sometimes your tribe has to throw the virgin into the volcano to appease the angry gods. Only Christianity has the Savior who gives you salvation according to His own work and sacrifice, not yours.

The other reason to ponder is this: remember that apart from Jesus, you're dead in sin. You can't do anything to earn salvation. If you had to do one little thing to get the forgiveness won by Jesus, you'd have no hope at all. In Him, you have every good gift of God—the kingdom of heaven is yours!

Which brings us to the next piece of the puzzle: how does Jesus get this forgiveness to you?

The Means

I don't know you personally, but I'm pretty sure you're not a time traveler. If you are, I'd like you to travel into the future and tell me if there's any hope of any sports team from Seattle winning a championship in my lifetime. If you're not, it means you can't travel back to Easter Sunday to see Jesus and hear Him forgive you. Neither can you make a quick trip up to heaven to get forgiveness from Him there. That leaves one option: He has to bring it to you somehow. How? Excellent question!

Suppose today is your birthday, and your good friend calls from the other side of the planet and says, "Hey, I've made a sculpture for you out of cotton balls and waffle batter. I'm looking at it right now, and it's yours! Happy Birthday!" Once you get past the gushy How-did-you-know-exactly-what-I-wanted? stage of the conversation, you get all practical and say, "Nuts! That sculpture might be mine, but it's at your place halfway around the world. It might be mine, but I don't have it."

52

"No problem," says your friend. He carefully wraps his creation in a box, ships it overnight, and pretty soon your doorbell is ringing. A cheerful man dressed in brown hands you the box. All of a sudden, things have changed: not only is the sculpture for you, but now you've got it in your hands.

Because you can't get up to heaven, Jesus takes the forgiveness He's won, wraps it in three different "packages," and sends them to you.

The Word

The first is His Word. God's Word isn't just informative, it's effective: it does what He says. How did He create the heavens and the earth? He spoke, and it happened, "And God said, 'Let there be light,' and there was light" (Genesis 1:3). Often, when Jesus healed people, He did so simply by speaking.

In fact, one of the all-time great Bible stories about this is in Mark 2. Jesus is teaching to a packed house in Capernaum. Four men bring their paralyzed friend on a bed; and when they can't get through the door, they lower him through the roof. We pick up the story there:

53

> And when Jesus saw their faith, He said to the paralytic, "Son, your sins are forgiven." Now some of the scribes were sitting there, questioning in their hearts, "Why does this man speak like that? He is blaspheming! Who can forgive sins but God alone?" And immediately Jesus, perceiving in His spirit that they thus questioned within themselves, said to them, "Why do you question these things in your hearts? Which is easier, to say to the paralytic, 'Your sins are forgiven,' or to say, 'Rise, take up your bed and walk'? But that you may know that the Son of Man has authority on earth to forgive sins"—He said to the paralytic—

"I say to you, rise, pick up your bed, and go home." And he rose and immediately picked up his bed and went out before them all, so that they were all amazed and glorified God, saying, "We never saw anything like this!" **(Mark 2:5–12)**

Jesus says two things to the paralytic. The first is, "Your sins are forgiven." This really ticks off the scribes, who immediately grumble that Jesus should only be saying that if He is God, which they don't believe Him to be. In response, Jesus demonstrates that He's God and that His Word is powerful stuff. He says the second thing to the paralytic, "Rise, pick up your bed, and go home." He speaks—that's all. But His Word is powerful enough to heal the man and send the man walking on his way.

For a brief experiment, try this at home. Take an object, like a pencil, this book, or a can of garbanzo beans. Put the object on a table. Step away, and speak to it. Tell it to move. Vary your volume and tone. Coax it. Command it. Scream at the top of your lungs at it.

You will discover two things from your experiment. One is that your neighbors will avoid you even more, since there was already a rumor going around that you talk to cows. The other is that you'll find that your word only informs, but doesn't effect—it doesn't cause things to happen. It can't make anything do squat.

Jesus' Word is effective. When Jesus said, "Rise," He gave healing to the man.

Likewise—and this is very important—when He said, "Your sins are forgiven," He gave forgiveness to the man.

So when you hear God's Word that you are forgiven, He's not informing you that somewhere along the way, you mysteriously run into an invisible cloud of grace; right there by His Word, He's giving you forgiveness.

Holy Baptism

Add water to the Word, and you get Holy Baptism. That's how Jesus instituted it in Matthew 28:19: "Go therefore and make disciples of all nations, baptizing [there's the water] them in the name of the Father and of the Son and of the Holy Spirit [that's the Word]." What does Baptism do? It forgives sins. That's what Peter declared in Acts 2:38: "And Peter said to them, 'Repent and be baptized every one of you in the name of Jesus Christ for the forgiveness of your sins, and you will receive the gift of the Holy Spirit.'" There you go: it's for the forgiveness of sins.

We'll look at Baptism more later on, and talk about why some Christians argue otherwise. But for now, we've established that Holy Baptism is one of the packages by which God delivers forgiveness to you.

Holy Communion

Add the Word to bread and wine, and we get to the third package: Holy Communion.

The setting was the Last Supper, as Jesus celebrated the Passover with His disciples . . .

> Now as they were eating, Jesus took bread, and after blessing it broke it and gave it to the disciples, and said, "Take, eat; this is My body." And He took a cup, and when He had given thanks He gave it to them, saying, "Drink of it, all of you, for this is My blood of the covenant, which is poured out for many for the forgiveness of sins." **(Matthew 26:26–28)**

In a mystery we can't understand, Jesus gives us His body and blood in, with, and under bread and wine. What is it for? Check out the end of the passage above. Specifically, Jesus gives us this Holy Communion "for the forgiveness of sins."

Again, we'll talk about Holy Communion later on, especially because it's a matter of controversy for many these days. But for now, we want to make clear that it's the third package the Lord uses to deliver forgiveness.

Properly Speaking . . .

If you look through the Small Catechism or other good Christian books, you won't find references to "packages that bring forgiveness." Rather, the Church has adopted the word *means*, as in an instrument used to accomplish something. For instance, my car is a *means* of transportation. The cactus in our backyard is a *means* of annoyance and unintended pain. God's Word, Holy Baptism, and Holy Communion are *means* by which God gives you forgiveness. That's why they're called "means of grace."

How does God work in these means? How can Baptism wash away sins? How can Jesus' body and blood be present in bread and wine? Those are mysteries. In Latin, a word for mystery is *sacramentum*. That's why Holy Baptism and Holy Communion are also called *Sacraments*. We can't explain precisely how God works in these means of grace—but we know He does because His Word says so.

Moving On . . .

So here's what we've established so far.

57

> * You were born dead in sin, not to
> mention blind, and an enemy of God.
> Therefore, you can't save yourself.
>
> * God sent His only Son, Jesus Christ,
> to die on the cross for your sin, in
> order to save you.

If only we could find a Bible verse to sum all of this up in a short way. . . . Wait—we can!

> For all have sinned and fall short of the
> glory of God, and are justified by His
> grace as a gift, through the redemp-
> tion that is in Christ Jesus.
> **(Romans 3:23–24)**

"All have sinned." That's pretty conclusive. If you jump back to verse 20, you'll also find the further information that no one gets rid of their sin by keeping God's Law, because they can't keep it. Furthermore, God's grace is a gift because Jesus paid the price—the redemption. He gives it to you since you can't get it or earn it yourself; and He gives it to you in His means of grace—His Word and Sacraments.

Now, this whole review of the Christian faith, especially salvation, is designed to lead us to some important questions about faith. A big one would be this: "If I'm dead in sin, how can I believe in Jesus?" That's a key question.

Right now, we'll answer a few other questions here, then move on to answer that one when we talk about faith in the next chapter.

Q&A:
You Ask . . .

i'm that sinful? i know i'm not perfect, but i don't feel that sinful.

I'd urge you not to go by what you feel. For one thing, consider the comparison earlier of a virus and its symptoms. It's possible to be physically sick without feeling any symptoms; likewise, the fact that you don't feel sinful doesn't mean you're not. Consider also the fact that sin makes you blind to what God says in His Word: this would mean your sinful nature is working hard to blind you to the fact that it's there.

More important, consider God's Word that says everyone is sinful (Romans 3:23 is pretty clear). Martin Luther put it this way in the

Small Catechism:

> To such person [who sees no need for forgiveness] no better advice can be given than this: first, he should touch his body to see if he still has flesh and blood. Then he should believe what the Scriptures say of it in **Galatians 5** and **Romans 7**. Second, he should look around to see whether he is still in the world, and remember that there will be no lack of sin and trouble, as the Scriptures say in **John 15–16** and in **1 John 2** and **5**. Third, he will certainly have the devil also around him, who with his lying and murdering day and night will let him have no peace, within or without, as the Scriptures picture him in **John 8** and **16**; **1 Peter 5**; **Ephesians 6**; and **2 Timothy 2**. (SC, p. 43)

In other words, he gives you a three-step check to see if you're a sinner in need of forgiveness: Are you (1) alive, (2) in this world, and (3) experiencing any sort of trouble or grief? If the answer is yes to any of the three, you need forgiveness.

if i try hard enough, can i stop sinning?

No. Some Christians still teach that you can become perfect in this life, but it isn't so. As long as you're in this world, you're still sinful. And as long as you're still sinful, you'll still sin. I think the best passage in Scripture is this honest confession by St. Paul in Romans 7:

> For I know that nothing good dwells in me, that is, in my flesh. For I have the desire to do what is right, but not the ability to carry it out. For I do not do the good I want, but the evil I do not want is what I keep on doing. Now if I do what I do not want, it is no longer I who do it, but sin that dwells within me. **(Romans 7:18–20)**

Paul goes on to describe the struggle between his old sinful nature and the new life Jesus has given him, and then he cries out, "Wretched man that I am! Who will deliver me from this body of death?" (Romans 7:24). Paul the apostle isn't approaching perfection—he's lamenting his sin! But what's his hope? He answers in verse 25, "Thanks be to God through Jesus Christ our Lord!" See, being a Christian isn't about working to be perfect, even though we should work hard at obeying God's Law (see Chapter 4, Faith and Good Works). Being a Christian is about rejoicing that you have a Savior who has taken away your sins and shared His perfect holiness with you (Romans 4:7–8).

Be careful, though; you can fool yourself into

61

thinking you're sinning less and getting better. It's not so. Instead, it means you've reduced your outward sins (like slugging your sister) and fallen prey to pride in your self-control instead. That's what the Pharisees did. Your sister might appreciate the change, but you're still sinning.

i'll admit it: i found this chapter pretty boring. i believe Jesus died on the cross to take away my sins. Why should i worry about all the rest of these details?

Maybe I should try that on my wife: "Honey, I believe your name is Teresa, so I really don't want to hear anything else about you." Or if she tries to tell me about her day, I can say, "Excuse me, but we're already married. That's all I really need to know about us, so don't tell me anything else." Yeah. That would work well.

I can also write with sarcasm.

Obviously, that's a shameful way to treat a loved one—why would it be any less shameful to treat Jesus the same way? He tells you who He is and what He's done for your good—for your salvation! As you learn more about Him, it strengthens your faith and confirms His love and faithfulness for you. The less you know about Jesus, the more likely you are to be led astray.

Another good question is this: if you're not seeking to know more about Jesus, what are you seeking to know more about? That stands a good chance of becoming a false god you care for more than your Savior.

I'll be honest, one of the greatest temptations Christians face today is indifference. (It's a tough sin to preach against, because indifferent people don't care what you say!) Thanks to the Web and cable television and podcasts and more, you're bombarded with far more information than you can absorb, and you'll always be tempted to focus on things that are practical or entertaining; everything else will seem boring and unimportant. The devil delights if you categorize your Savior as boring and unimportant. It betrays a lack of love and a shaky faith.

When people are indifferent to the Gospel, they don't realize their sin unless the Lord makes use of some trial to show them their need. I'd advise against you taking that chance. Repent of indifference now, and make it a point to learn more about your Savior. You'll never exhaust your study or the wonder of who Jesus is.

Oh, and rejoice in this too—Jesus already knows exactly who you are—which is why He died for you, and He continues to love you anyway!

My friend says the Trinity isn't biblical, and points to Deuteronomy 6:4: "Hear, O israel: The Lord our God, the Lord is one." if God is one, how can He be three?

I can't explain the Trinity, and a lengthy discussion is too much for this book. However, I will say Deuteronomy 6:4 doesn't contradict the Trinity. That word for *one* can mean "one thing composed of more than one part." For instance, it's found in Genesis 2:24: "Therefore a man shall leave his father and his mother and hold fast to his wife, and they shall become *one* flesh" (emphasis mine). Man and wife become *one* flesh—but aren't they still *two* distinct persons? Likewise, we worship one God, who reveals Himself as three distinct persons— Father, Son, and Holy Spirit.

When did Jesus save me—at the cross, or when i was baptized?

The answer is yes. Jesus won salvation for

you by His death on the cross. He gave that salvation to you in Baptism. (If you want the technical jargon, Jesus' death for the whole world is called *objective justification*, while His giving salvation specifically to you is *subjective justification*.) Does this matter? It can when you're in a conversation. If someone insists that Jesus didn't save her until she decided to believe in Him, then I might gently say that Jesus saved us long before we were born. On the other hand, if someone claims everyone is saved because Jesus died for all, then I'm going to make sure to bring up the truth that He saves individuals through His means of grace.

65

At church, we say Jesus was "Begotten of the Father from eternity." So what was Jesus doing before He was born to Mary?

He was busy preparing the way for His death and resurrection. Often when we read of the LORD at work in the Old Testament, we simply assume we're reading about God the Father. But why? Why would it not be Jesus (He is Lord, after all) who appeared to Moses in the burning bush (Exodus 3:2) or led the people of Israel out of Egypt (Exodus 13:21)? If the LORD was there, Jesus was there.

What does "begotten" mean, anyway? isn't it just an old word nobody uses anymore?

Actually, it's a pretty important word with significant meaning: it's the man's side of producing offspring. In other words, women *bear* children and men *beget* children. To say that Jesus was begotten—not born—from eternity declares that He is of the Father without a mother; He's born of Mary in Bethlehem much later.

66

i have friends who aren't Christians. They don't seem like "enemies of God" to me.

Given how we usually use the word *enemy* I can understand. But consider this: there are those who believe in Jesus and those who do not. Those who don't believe in Jesus believe in something else. They might believe there is no God. They might believe there's a different god that saves. They might believe they save themselves by their own work of being a pretty good person, or that they're just too sinful to be forgiven, or something else. That's a wide range of beliefs, but they all have this in common: they all say, "I don't want Jesus and the forgiveness He's won for me." All those beliefs, whether stated with hostility or warmth, say no to the Gospel.

Sometimes, when people visit our church, i hear them called seekers. What does this mean?

I think we want to be careful with that term. I've heard it used to imply that there are just some people who are seeking out God long before they hear His Word. But the Scriptures are clear: "No one seeks for God" (Romans 3:11). One can only come to the Father through the Son (1 John 2:23), and one only believes in the Son by faith—the faith the Word gives. Therefore, you can't be seeking God until you've heard the Word.

On the other hand, those who visit a church may have heard the Word and want to know more about Jesus, so the Holy Spirit is gathering them in. Or perhaps they're looking for something, good or bad; in that sense, I suppose, they're seekers—though we don't know what exactly they're seeking. Whoever they

67

are and whatever the reason they're there, we want to tell them all about Jesus and His death on the cross. (See section 5, Faith and Worship, for more.) But let's be clear: the Bible only speaks of believers and unbelievers. It doesn't mention a middle ground of people who are seeking after the one true God apart from His work and Word.

You quoted Genesis 8:21 that "the intention of man's heart is evil from his youth." Aren't kids innocent—at least more innocent than adults?

68

Children will appear more innocent than adults, since they haven't had the time to learn and experience all the crummy stuff adults have gotten into. But alas, kids aren't innocent. In fact, the Bible makes clear that all of us are sinful from the time we're conceived (Psalm 51:5); and anyone who's spent time with a baby knows that sometimes a baby cries just for self-ish attention. There isn't a time we don't need a Savior—but there isn't a time Jesus hasn't saved us!

But does God hold babies accountable for sin? What about an age of accountability?

Some Christians teach that there's an age of accountability—in other words, while children are sinful, God doesn't hold their sins against them until they reach a certain age or level of maturity. This is largely based on the teaching that children reach an "age of reason" or "age of discretion," at which they finally comprehend what is morally right and wrong. It's true that minds mature over time, and children are able to comprehend more. However, the Bible never says children are not sinful or accountable for sin until a certain age.

The Bible does acknowledge a tragic proof that children are sinful and accountable for sin. "The wages of sin is death," says Romans 6:23: people die because they are sinful. Children die—therefore, children are sinful. It's a stark, unhappy truth. But it's still true. That's why we rejoice that Jesus didn't die only for adults, but for all people of all nations—infants included.

Why would Christians teach an "age of accountability"? Because it has to do with a misunderstanding about faith. Some believe faith is something we do—therefore, to have faith, you have to be old enough to understand

69

what you believe. Therefore, God must have a special provision for children who aren't old enough to believe or to understand. In the next couple of sections we'll see that faith isn't something we do to reach God; rather, it's a gift God gives to us—and to infants too.

You used the word learnified. is that really a word?

You caught me. I meant to say *smartified*.

My friend is serious about studying religion. He says Calvin is right and Luther is wrong about salvation. Can you fill me in?

Let's talk for a minute about three men: John Calvin, Martin Luther, and Jacob Arminius. All three were very smart guys and serious about theology. Each has come to represent one view about salvation and faith.

Calvin took the position that God does all the work to save and to damn. This view, sometimes called *double predestination*, says God chooses some to be saved, but also chooses others to be damned. According to Calvinism, when Jesus died for all, He died for all whom

70

you ask about . . . FAITH

God would choose to be saved, but not for those who would be damned. When it comes to salvation, then, you're either in or you're out. God's already decided. For Calvin, faith is like a tattoo—it's something God puts on those whom He's chosen to save.

Arminius took the opposite view of Calvin. He stated that man has free will to choose to be saved or to be damned. If man decides to believe in Jesus, he gets forgiveness and heaven. If man chooses to reject Jesus, then he's condemned himself. Either way, salvation is determined by man, not God. For Arminius, faith is something man has on his own—he can choose to believe in Jesus.

So far, Calvin has said God chooses to save or to damn, and Arminius has said man chooses whether to be saved or be damned.

In between, you find Luther, who said if you get to heaven, it's all God's doing and none of your own. But if you get to hell, it's all your own fault. How can this be?

Because you start out dead. Remember Deadguy on the stretcher in the ER, who's dead and can't save himself? The doctors come along and bring him to life. Now he's alive—not by his work, but by the work of others. Let's say, though, that Deadguy doesn't want to be alive, so he goes running out of the hospital and jumps off a bridge and into the sea of sharks below. Why is Deadguy dead again? Because he threw away the gift of life he'd been given.

Luther steadfastly maintained that we were dead in sin. It's the Lord who makes us alive by giving us forgiveness—therefore, salvation and life are all His doing, not ours. If we reject it—if we say "I don't believe in Jesus" or "I'd rather keep the sin and not be forgiven," then we're lost again—and that's completely our fault.

This is astonishing: every time people hear the Gospel, Jesus is giving them forgiveness and life and salvation. If they believe it, it's all because He's given it to them—faith included. If they reject it, that's their doing, not His—because God desires all to be saved (1 Timothy 2:4).

So how come some believe in Jesus and others reject Him?

That's the question we can't answer. Calvin thought he could by saying, "Because God chose some to be saved and some to be lost." Arminius thought he could by saying, "Because God gave people free will, and each one makes the choice." To me, that's what makes their ideas so attractive—they can answer that question, even if their ideas don't agree with Scripture.

We don't know why some believe and others do not. We can't even say that those who believe are saved because they resist God less than others, because that would mean they were earning salvation by not fighting as much. It's a mystery, and a difficult one to accept. However, you find this happening repeatedly in the Bible. In the Old Testament, God chose the people of Israel to be His. They didn't do anything special to earn His favor. In fact, God chose them before they existed. He picked Abraham and said, "I'm going to make you the father of a great nation" (see Genesis 22:17). Did the people of Israel choose to be God's people? No. He chose them. Yet, again and again, the chosen people chose to reject God and turn to false gods that couldn't save (see Judges 10:10 and Jeremiah 2:28). Why? There's no good reason, they were tempted to reject God, and they did.

Salvation is a gift. By definition, a gift can be refused. At the cost of Jesus' blood, God gives salvation to all. Blinded by sin, some reject the gift and are lost. But of this you can be sure: because God does desire all to be saved (1 Timothy 2:4), you can be certain He will save all who would believe in Him.

73

Why does God send people to hell?

Given what we've already talked about, the short and easy answer is that God sentences people to hell because they reject Jesus and the forgiveness He's won.

However, this is worth exploring more, so I ask you this question: do those who don't believe in Jesus want to be in heaven? Consider what we know from Scripture.

We know that when sinners get anywhere near God in His glory, they don't want to get any closer. One example would be Israel at Mount Sinai. When God descended on the top of Sinai to be close to His people, they weren't thrilled. Instead, they begged Moses, "You speak to us, and we will listen; but do not let God speak to us, lest we die" (Exodus 20:19). We can look at other examples. When Adam and Eve fell into sin, they hid from God (Genesis 3:8); after Cain murdered Abel, he "went away from the presence of the LORD" (Genesis 4:16). In the New Testament, we hear the story of the rich man and Lazarus, where the rich man is in hell. What does he ask for— deliverance? No. He asks for a drink of water (Luke 16:24). He expresses no desire to move toward heaven, even though he does hope that his brothers might still repent.

At present, the Lord comes mercifully, hidden in His Word and Sacraments to declare grace. On the Last Day, He will appear in glory—why would those who want to hide from Him now want to be near Him then? Indeed, Revelation records that those who have rejected Christ will cry out,

> Fall on us and hide us from the face
> of Him who is seated on the throne,
> and from the wrath of the Lamb, for
> the great day of their wrath has come,
> and who can stand?
> **(Revelation 6:16–17)**

Please understand, whether the fire of hell is real or an abstract description (there's a lot of debate about this), hell will not be a pleasant place to be. At the same time, there's no evidence in Scripture that those within it will want to be in heaven.

Do all Christians believe God gives forgiveness in the Sacraments?

No. Many Christians see Baptism and Communion as mere symbols and little more. We're going to talk about this later on, but this is important: what you believe about faith and salvation will directly determine what you believe about the Sacraments. That's why

75

we're going to spend a few pages looking at what faith is before we talk about Baptism and Communion. We'll get back to the Sacraments when we talk about faith and worship.

You said forgiveness is a gift. But i have to repent before God gives me forgiveness, right?

Be careful. Repentance is necessary, but it's not something you do. If repentance was something you do, then you'd have to do something to earn forgiveness and forgiveness wouldn't be a gift. Plus, you can't repent on your own: you're Deadguy, remember?

Here's better news from the Bible. Repentance is a gift, along with forgiveness. Peter makes this clear in Acts 5:31: "God exalted Him at His right hand as Leader and Savior, to give repentance to Israel and forgiveness of sins." (See also 2 Timothy 2:25.)

But i have to believe before i'm forgiven . . . right?

No. You're Deadguy before you're forgiven, and the dead can't believe or do anything else. It's time to turn the page and learn more about faith.

Section Two:
The Basics
78 of Faith

The first time I was teaching youth about faith, I thought an illustration would help. I decided to draw what faith looked like. So I mustered all of my artistic skills, took a deep breath, and drew.

Of the students in class, one of them coughed. Another rolled her eyes. A third said, in a disturbed sort of way, "That looks like a stick figure with a funnel stuck in his head."

I wasn't sure what to think. On the one hand, I was disappointed by the overall lack of appreciation. On the other hand, I was relieved—I'm not much of an artist, but at least one of them actually recognized that I was trying to draw a stick figure with a funnel stuck in his head.

Still, it was a silly little picture; and now, after years of being a pastor, I wouldn't use it again. No, instead I would draw a stick figure with a funnel that had hands reaching up, and it would be stuck in his ear. I'm just not sure I could ever pull off an illustration that complex. I just tried it, and the dog yelped and ran into her crate. For the sake of us all, I'm glad there's a shredder nearby.

"A funnel with hands reaching up, stuck in someone's ear?" you ask politely, as you wonder if you still have the receipt for this book.

79

"Oui," I respond, trying to sound all French and cultured. Perhaps I'd best explain. This chapter will introduce you to two really big, important truths about faith—and give you one important verse to remember for each one.

Two Big Truths about Faith

1. Faith is a gift of the Holy Spirit.

Faith is a gift that God gives to you. Here's

one of the most important verses you'll find in the Bible about faith:

"For by grace you have been saved through faith. And this is not your own doing; it is the gift of God, not a result of works, so that no one may boast" (Ephesians 2:8–9).

That's pretty clear. Faith is a gift of God. It's "not your own doing," and it's "not a result of works."

Many get this wrong and believe that faith is something you do—something you have without God's help. But that simply can't be. Why? I offer three arguments from what we've studied about salvation—because faith and salvation go together.

First, you're dead, remember? A dead man can't bring himself to life, and faith brings life and salvation (Acts 16:31). If you're dead in your sin, you can't do the work of believing any more than the heart-attack victim can take those paddles and defibrillate himself back to life. That's why 1 Corinthians 2:14 says, "The natural person does not accept the things of the Spirit of God, for they are folly to him, and he is not able to understand them because they are spiritually discerned." The natural person—an unforgiven sinner—doesn't accept the things of the Spirit of God: he doesn't believe. He can't.

Therefore, if you have faith, it's because it was given to you.

Second, you're an enemy of God, right? Remember Romans 8:7, "For the mind that is set on the flesh is hostile to God, for it does not submit to God's law; indeed, it cannot." As an enemy of God, you naturally resist Him—you don't trust Him. As the verse says, you can't submit and trust. Therefore, if you have faith, it's because it's been given to you.

Third, we've also established from the Bible that Jesus has done everything to save you. We didn't say, "Jesus has done everything to save you, except that you have to do the work of believing." If Jesus truly has done everything to save you, then giving you faith is something He does. It's not something you do.

Faith "is the gift of God" (Ephesians 2:8). To be precise, it is a gift the Holy Spirit gives to you. That's a truth worth backing up with a couple of Scripture passages:

> Now we have received not the spirit of the world, but the Spirit who is from God, that we might understand the things freely given us by God.
> **(1 Corinthians 2:12)**

> Therefore I want you to understand that no one speaking in the Spirit of God ever says "Jesus is accursed!" and

81

> no one can say "Jesus is Lord" except
> in the Holy Spirit.
> **(1 Corinthians 12:3)**

Clearly, it's the Holy Spirit who gives us faith to believe. What's more, 1 Corinthians 12:3 makes clear that He gives us faith to believe in Jesus. That leads us to another important point about faith.

The job of faith is to receive what God gives.

What does this gift of faith do? It believes. Faith is the trust in God's promise that your sins are forgiven for Jesus' sake. By trusting God's promise of forgiveness, faith receives the forgiveness God gives. And if you are forgiven for your sins, then you also have life in Christ—faith believes that and receives it too. Furthermore, if you're forgiven, you also have salvation. You're no longer enslaved in sin. Faith believes this too—so faith receives salvation.

To put it another way, faith grabs the forgiveness that Jesus promises, and therefore you're forgiven. Faith believes God saves you and holds onto that salvation, and so it's yours. Faith reaches out and grasps the eternal life Christ has won, so you're going to live forever.

That's why I drew faith as a funnel on a

stick man's head in class. Jesus died for the sins of the whole world. For His sake, God the Father showers this world with forgiveness, life, and salvation. Those who have the funnel stuck in their heads (those who have faith) fill up with grace and life. Those who don't have the funnel stuck in their heads (those who don't have faith) simply let these gifts of God bounce off them and fall to the ground.

Faith receives the gifts of God. Without it, you can't be forgiven or saved or alive. Again, this makes perfect sense as long as we've got a scriptural understanding of salvation. If you're dead in sin, you need this gift of faith to receive forgiveness and life for you.

83

We need to clarify one more thing about this gift: faith isn't passive. It's active because it clings to Jesus.

A funnel is a passive thing. It just sits in the drawer or on the counter and does nothing until it's used. It doesn't do tricks or wash your car. If you were to stick an actual funnel into your head—and I am by no means suggesting that you do—you would find that (a) it would hurt a lot, and (b) it would do nothing but hurt a lot and catch whatever things happened to fall into it accidentally.

That's where the funnel breaks down as an

illustration of faith. Faith doesn't just sit like a funnel and catch whatever belief comes your way. Rather, faith focuses only on Jesus. It clings to the Savior who died on the cross for you, because He's the only source of forgiveness. Whenever other, false teachings come your way, faith is busy batting them away and clinging to Jesus.

That's why, if I were to draw it all over again, I'd draw faith as a funnel with hands—hands that hold on to the Good News of Jesus on the cross. That's what faith does.

Once again, this only makes sense if you've got the Gospel right, since you're dead in sin and salvation is found only in Jesus. Faith clings to life, so it clings to Jesus and nothing else.

So faith is a gift of God that holds on to for-giveness and life for you. This leads us to an important question. Where do you get it? How do you get it? This leads us to the next important truth.

2. God gives you faith in His Word.

Exhibit A:

"So faith comes from hearing, and hearing through the word of Christ" (Romans 10:17).

The same Good News that brings forgiveness also brings faith. Forgiveness and faith always go together: you can't believe unless you're forgiven, and you're not forgiven unless you believe. As we saw in the previous chapter, with forgiveness comes every good gift from God—and faith is one of them.

Working backwards, we get to Exhibit B: what keeps you from having faith—from trusting in God? Sin is what makes you dead (Romans 6:23) and keeps you from trusting God's Word. Without sin, you'd naturally believe in Jesus and gladly receive all those things He's promised. What removes sin? Forgiveness does. And if your sin is taken away, what prevents you from believing? Nothing. With forgiveness comes faith—and faith comes by hearing through the Word of Christ. This, by the way, is why I'd have the funnel with the hands stuck in the stick figure's ear if I were to draw the picture again.

In fact, the ear is a pretty good example of a funnel all by itself. You don't have to make an effort to hear—you hear things all the time, whether you want to or not. Your ears just take in the sounds that are sent your way. Likewise, faith gladly takes in the forgiveness God sends in His Word and in His Sacraments. Faith isn't like eyes that you open and close. It's like ears

85

that are constantly working to receive—with one big difference. Faith doesn't just passively receive whatever comes its way. It actively grabs only what Jesus promises.

Weak Faith and Strong Faith

In the Bible, Jesus talks about weak faith and strong faith. In Matthew 14:31, He says to Peter, "O you of little faith, why did you doubt?" On the other hand, one chapter later He says to the Canaanite woman, "O woman, great is your faith! Be it done for you as you desire" (Matthew 15:28). Faith is stronger in some people than in other people. Your faith will be strong at times and weak at other times. It fluctuates.

But here's the thing: whether it's weak or strong, it's still saving faith. Faith clings to Jesus, right? And even when it's weak, it still clings to the same Jesus—and Jesus isn't weak. In other words, God doesn't give you weak forgiveness when your faith is weak and strong forgiveness when your faith is strong: He always gives the same, sufficient grace to take away all of your sins.

Now, strong faith is better than weak faith—no doubt about that. The one who has strong faith will be able to resist more temptation, perform more good works, and rejoice more in the promises and gifts of God. But whether it's weak or strong, faith holds on to Jesus.

Let's use the example of a heartbeat. Remember Deadguy in Chapter 1, on the stretcher in the ER? He's either dead or alive, his heart is either beating or it's not. The doctors aren't going to say he's "mostly dead" or "sort of alive-ish." If his heart is beating, he's alive. However, a strong heartbeat is far better than a weak heartbeat.

Faith is the same way; one either believes or he does not. If his faith is weak, he still has life in Christ. However, a strong faith is far better than a weak faith. That's why it's so important continually to hear God's Word and receive His Supper; as He gives you forgiveness, He feeds and strengthens your faith.

This is very important, because faith can die. In Luke 8:13, Jesus warns that some will gladly receive the Word and believe it for a while (that's faith in action!), but then they will fall away. Why does this happen? One reason is neglect. The less people feed their faith with God's Word and forgiveness, the weaker their faith becomes. And just like their physical bodies, they'll have a tougher time warding off attacks when their faith is weak.

In the case of Luke 8:13, people fall away because they face a "time of testing," perhaps persecution or some sickness or tragedy. Certainly the devil will use such things to try to convince you that God doesn't love you, that faith is useless, and that you might as well give it up and look after yourself instead of trusting Jesus.

There are other enemies of faith, though. 1 Timothy 4:1 declares that some will depart from the faith to follow false teachings. Don't be deceived, your sinful flesh is going to be attracted to any religion that doesn't proclaim the Gospel, because only the Gospel takes away sin and destroys your sinful flesh. Throughout your life, you'll find yourself tempted to buy into other religions—or at least soften up God's Word to make room for other teachings. But faith clings to the one true Jesus; and when you embrace other teachings, you're causing your faith to loosen its grip on Christ. Beware, some of the most seductive false teachings don't come from religions on the outside—they come from your sinful heart. Daily, you'll be tempted to follow what you want, rather than what God says.

This leads us to another faith-killer—willful sin. We all sin every day, even when we're trying hard not to. But it's a dangerous thing to sin on purpose. When you do so, you say, "I like this sin, so I don't want this sin taken away. Therefore, I don't want to be forgiven. I don't want Jesus to take away this sin." When you do that, you're telling faith to take a hike. That means you're back to being dead in sin and lost for eternity.

Can people who have completely lost faith get it back? Absolutely! Just because they're dead doesn't mean God has changed. He still offers forgiveness to them—and every time they hear the Gospel, God is offering faith again. All of this is summed up in one of my favorite passages:

89

> The saying is trustworthy, for: If we have died with Him, we will also live with Him; if we endure, we will also reign with Him; if we deny Him, He also will deny us; if we are faithless, He remains faithful—for He cannot deny Himself. **(2 Timothy 2:11–13)**

"If we have died with Him, we also will live with Him." How do we die with Christ? In Baptism, (Romans 6:3–4), where God gives us forgiveness and faith. Therefore, we live with Him because we have faith.

"If we endure, we also will reign with Him." Because we—by faith—cling to Jesus, we will reign with Him forever. There's no doubt. The only way we could possibly not reign with Him would be to throw our faith away.

"If we deny Him, He will deny us." If we abandon our faith, cling to sin, and deny He is our Savior, He will deny that we are His people.

"If we are faithless, He remains faithful—for He cannot deny Himself." But even if we are faithless because we threw faith away the Lord hasn't changed. He remains faithful to His promises, and faithfully seeks to restore us with forgiveness again. Having paid the price of His own blood, Jesus will not give up on us now.

90

In this chapter, we looked at two gigantic, important truths about faith. If nothing else, remember especially these two Bible passages:

> For by grace you have been saved through faith. And this is not your own doing; it is the gift of God, not a result of works, so that no one may boast. (Ephesians 2:8–9)

> So faith comes from hearing, and hearing through the word of Christ. (Romans 10:17)

From those two verses you know that faith is a gift of God, and you know that He gives it to you in His Word. If you keep those two truths straight, you're well on your way to being able to discern truths and errors about faith. When people start teaching the wrong things about faith, it's usually because they've messed up one of those two truths.

For the sake of review, I'll draw one more picture for you.

Picture, if you will, a boat in the middle of the sea. As it continues on course, the sailor on watch reports a man floating face down in the water, and the alarm bell sounds. Rescue crews take their stations, tie a rope to a life ring, and throw it into the water. It lands right next to the man, but it's not enough. Why? Because the guy is face down—by all appearances, he's dead. He can't reach out and grab the ring. His salvation is right next to him, but he still isn't rescued. In fact, the crew could throw a million life rings into the water, and the guy would still be a goner. Something more has to be done. In this case, a sailor has to jump overboard and swim to the man. He grabs the rope in one hand, the man in the other, and gives the signal to pull; and he holds on to both until they've been pulled safely on deck, where the ship's surgeon miraculously revives the victim.

Now, all analogies break down sooner or later, so don't push the story too far. The guy in the water is you—dead in sin. As people tell

91

you the Gospel that Jesus died for your sins, they're hurling salvation at you—but because you're dead in sin, you can't do anything to grab it. That's where faith comes in. The Holy Spirit sends faith, and faith is like the guy who jumps in and ties you to the life ring, then sticks around to make sure the knots stay tight. That's what faith does—it grabs God's gifts of forgiveness and life for you.

Faith is a gift of God, given by the Holy Spirit in the Gospel so you receive forgiveness, life, and salvation. As we close this section on the basics of faith, one more passage:

> God chose you as the firstfruits to be saved, through sanctification by the Spirit and belief in the truth. To this He called you through our gospel, so that you may obtain the glory of our Lord Jesus Christ.
> **(2 Thessalonians 2:13–14)**

For Jesus' sake, God chose you and sent the Holy Spirit, who sanctified you—made you holy—by the Gospel, which means He gave you forgiveness and faith. Rejoice, my friend, the whole Holy Trinity is at work to save you.

Questions?

Q&A:
You Ask . . .

You quoted Ephesians 2:8–9,
"For by grace you have been saved
through faith. . . . it is the gift of God."
So which one is the gift of God—grace,
faith, or salvation?

It's a package deal. If you have forgiveness, you have salvation, right? Is it possible to be forgiven and not be saved? No, thanks be to God; that would put us all in doubt of our salvation. Can you have forgiveness without faith? No! No one can say, "I don't believe in Jesus, but He forgives me." And seeing as how you're

Deadguy, both faith and forgiveness must be gifts God gives to save you.

instead of a funnel with hands reaching out, why wouldn't you draw a funnel with tentacles?

Because that would just be creepy.

My friend says i have to accept Jesus as my personal Savior and Lord to be saved. What does this mean?

94 Remember that quick discussion of Luther, Calvin, and Arminius in the previous chapter? Your friend is interpreting Scripture like Arminius. Sometimes this is called *decision theology*, which teaches that you have to decide to follow Jesus in order to be forgiven. This is popular in a lot of churches today. You might hear it in words such as, "Jesus wants to forgive you—if you just ask Him to," or something as cornball as "Jesus and the devil have each cast a vote for your soul, and it's up to you to cast the deciding vote!" Churches that promote this theology often have an "altar call" during the service so people can "make a decision" for Jesus.

What's the problem? You can't do it. No one can decide to follow Jesus because we're all dead until He forgives us and makes us alive. By making us alive, He makes us His followers. Rejoice! Long ago, Jesus made the decision to be born and to die in order to save you!

Does it matter? Are there consequences to decision theology?

There are. For one thing, it denies the basic truth that we're born dead in sin and can do nothing to save ourselves. It turns faith into our work rather than God's gift—and why would it ever be smart to take credit for what God does?

There are practical consequences too. If you believe that you're saved in part because you decided to follow Jesus, how can you be sure your decision was good enough? As we already heard in Jeremiah 17:9, you can't even trust your own heart—if faith is your work, how can you ever be sure you really accepted Jesus, and you're not just fooling yourself? You might argue, "Because I'm not committing the same sins as I was before." But there's going to be a day when you do, and then you won't be sure

95

anymore. You might say, "Because life isn't as difficult as it was before," but there will be days when it will be worse. As soon as you say that you have to accept Jesus to be saved, you've introduced doubt into your salvation.

Another consequence is this: decision theology messes up your understanding of the means of grace. Take, for instance, Holy Baptism. God gives forgiveness, faith, and salvation in Holy Baptism. (We'll look at this more in section 5, Faith and Worship.) That doesn't work in decision theology, though. In that scheme, you get forgiveness and salvation because of your act of believing and accepting Jesus. Therefore, decision theology teaches that Baptism is not God's work to give you salvation; rather, it's your work to show your commitment to God. Look at that—Holy Baptism is turned from God's work on you to your work for God. Is that twisted or what?

Decision theology is popular. In fact, it rules contemporary Christian music today; so if you listen to Christian rock or pop, you're going to think it's the only teaching out there. But *popular* does not mean *right*. It's bad news to believe you have to do something to be forgiven, to accept Jesus. It's Good News that Jesus has forgiven and accepted you.

96

Wait a minute. In the book of Acts, when people asked Peter what they should do to be forgiven, Peter told people to "Repent and be baptized" (Acts 2:38). Later on in Acts 16, a jailer asked Paul and Silas, "What must I do to be saved?" and they said, "Believe in the Lord Jesus, and you will be saved, you and your household" (Acts 16:31). The apostles told people to believe. Isn't this proof that faith is our work— that we need to believe to be saved?

This is a GREAT question! It sounds like the apostles are telling the people to do something, doesn't it? But your antennae—and maybe your tentacles—are twitching because you know that every last one of those people is Deadguy, and Deadguy can't do anything!

Remember (section 1) that God's Word is effective—it does what it says. He said "Let there be light," and there was light. Jesus spoke to people and healed them, in effect saying, "Let there be healing," and there was. Think back to the story of Lazarus, who died four days before Jesus arrived at his home. Jesus went to the tomb and said, "Lazarus, come out" (John 11:43). He didn't say, "Lazarus, if you decide to come out, I'll make you alive." Instead, by that Word, Jesus gave him life and the power to walk out of the tomb.

In Acts 2, Peter has just preached a sermon about Jesus. In other words, he's just preached God's faith-giving Word. Then he says, "Repent and be baptized every one of you in the name of Jesus Christ for the forgiveness of your sins, and you will receive the gift of the Holy Spirit" (Acts 2:38). When Peter says "repent," it's like Jesus saying, "Lazarus, come out." He's not telling the people what to do on their own. Just as Jesus gave Lazarus life by His Word, Peter is giving the people repentance by God's Word!

It's the same with Paul and Silas in Acts 16. They tell the jailer to believe in Jesus, and then go on to tell him and his family more of God's Word about Jesus. That Word gives them faith; they believe because God's Word is giving them faith to believe.

The technical term (for use in impressing your pastor) is *evangelical imperative* or *Gospel imperative*. It's a command of God that gives forgiveness. It's not like a command of the Law, such as "Thou shalt not bear false witness against thy neighbor," which tells you what to do but gives you no power to do it. A Gospel imperative tells you what to do (repent, believe, etc.) and gives it (repentance, faith, etc.) to you

you ask about . . . FAITH

at the same time.

if faith is a gift of God, it would be pretty silly for me to boast about how strong my faith is, wouldn't it?

Some people do, but you and I (and they!) have no right to boast about our faith as if it's something we've come up with. It's not as if God looked down on you and me and said, "Wow, they really believe, so I'm going to save them." Again, faith and salvation are God's work for Jesus' sake. Paul sums this up in Romans 3:

99

> Then what becomes of our boasting? It is excluded. By what kind of law? By a law of works? No, but by the law of faith. For we hold that one is justified by faith apart from works of the law.
> **(Romans 3:27–28)**

As Deadguy, we have nothing to boast about in ourselves, because it's Jesus who does the saving. We don't do anything. That's why Paul adds later, "Let the one who boasts, boast in the Lord" (1 Corinthians 1:31). It's good that we speak not of ourselves, but of what Jesus has done. When we do so, we're proclaiming the Gospel—the Gospel that gives forgiveness and faith to those who can hear us talking.

is it proper to say i'm saved by faith?

It depends on what you mean. If you're saying you're saved because God has given you faith so you trust you're forgiven for Jesus' sake, then yes. If you're saying you're saved because you've decided to believe in Jesus, then no.

is it true that salvation can't be lost? i've heard the phrase "once saved, always saved."

Some churches teach that you can't lose salvation once you've got it. This is based on passages such as John 10:27–29, where Jesus says,

> My sheep hear My voice, and I know them, and they follow Me. I give them eternal life, and they will never perish, and no one will snatch them out of My hand. My Father, who has given them to Me, is greater than all, and no one is able to snatch them out of the Father's hand.

The argument goes, "Once you have faith and salvation, you can't lose them. So if one who is a Christian forsakes the faith, he never had faith in the first place."

There are problems with this. For one thing, there are examples of believers who had eternal life, but lost it. The first and obvious example is Adam and Eve, who were created to live forever until they sinned. Solomon would be another one; as king, he clearly had faith in God (1 Kings 3:3), but later rejected Him for idols (1 Kings 11:9–10). In the parable of the sower, Jesus tells of those who receive the Word with joy (that's what faith does, right?) and endure for a while, but then fall away because of hardship or persecution (Matthew 13:20–21).

Furthermore, the writer of Hebrews warns:

101

> For it is impossible, in the case of those who have once been enlightened, who have tasted the heavenly gift, and have shared in the Holy Spirit, and have tasted the goodness of the Word of God and the powers of the age to come, and then have fallen away, to restore them again to repentance, since they are crucifying once again the Son of God to their own harm and holding Him up to contempt. **(Hebrews 6:4–6)**

Clearly, it's possible for a Christian to reject faith and forfeit salvation.

Remember, faith is a gift. Gifts don't force or coerce—otherwise, they're not gifts anymore.

Let's say I give my wife a pair of earrings that look like Twinkies—actual size and everything. They're a gift, and she can do with them what she pleases. But if I force her to wear them every day, then they're not a gift anymore. It's become a matter of coercion. Faith and grace are gifts. God doesn't force anyone to be saved. If He did, salvation wouldn't be a gift anymore. It would be slavery.

Don't forget the good news of John 10:27–29, though. It's absolutely true that nothing is strong enough to override the forgiveness Jesus gives you—the forgiveness you freely receive by faith.

102

i'm afraid i've committed an unforgivable sin that Jesus won't forgive me for. Can i be forgiven?

The fact that you're concerned means God has not forsaken you. As we mentioned in the section 1 Q&A section, repentance is a gift of God. If He weren't still with you and giving you repentance, you wouldn't care about this at all.

The unforgivable sin is defined by Jesus as "[blaspheming] the Holy Spirit" in Mark 3:29. To *blaspheme* the Holy Spirit is to speak evil of Him or to slander Him. What does the Holy Spirit do? He gives you faith in Jesus (1 Corinthians 12:3). To speak evil of the Holy Spirit is, first and foremost, to reject what the Holy Spirit gives you—faith and forgiveness. Thus Hebrews 10:29 says that to spurn Jesus is to outrage the Holy Spirit. If you reject forgiveness, then you're not forgiven. That's the unforgivable sin.

So confess your sin, and be sure of this: Jesus died for you and you're forgiven.

You quoted Hebrews 6:4–6 a couple questions ago, which said that some can never be forgiven. Who is that talking about?

That text is quite the sober warning, because it describes those who were once strong Christians, but have now reached the point where it's "impossible" for them to be forgiven. Why is it impossible? Because they now hold Jesus in contempt instead of trusting in Him for forgiveness; they don't want Him and His grace anymore. They're looking elsewhere for help and salvation. As long as that's the case, it's impossible for them to be saved.

Does every sin destroy my faith?

No. Every sin works against your faith, but not every sin destroys it.

Think of it this way: my wife and I have two sons, who inherited the same sinful flesh we have. They're great kids, but they're not perfect; sometimes, they disobey. When one of them does something wrong, I don't say, "That's it! You're out of the family." He's still my son. I might have to sit on him for a while, but he's still in the family. In fact, the only way he's not going to be part of the family is if he runs away from home.

God has brought you into His family by grace. You're not a slave in God's house, but a son and an heir of His kingdom (Galatians 4:7). Even though you're a child of God, you're still going to sin—but Jesus died for those sins, right? That's why you confess your sin and rejoice that you're still in the family.

Confession is important, because every sin works to make you reject your Savior, to make you run away from home. It might be a matter of temptations that seem fun or pleasurable, such as drug abuse or sexual temptation. These sins are designed to make you say, "I'd rather have these sins and eternal death than Jesus and life, so I'm willing to forfeit my salvation and run away from home." It might be sins of doubt because of trouble, where you're tempted to say, "My life is going so poorly that I'm going to look for another god who treats me better as his kid." It might be all sorts of cares that distract you from Jesus and His Word until you just wander away from home and don't come back. Willful, premeditated sins (as opposed to sins committed ignorantly) are especially damaging to faith, because they involve a deliberate rejection of God's Word.

Another example would be Noah's family during the flood (Genesis 7). Did they remain sinless throughout the voyage? I'm betting the answer is no. (Put me in a tent with my family for one day of rain, and we're about ready to strangle each other!) But did they stay in the ark? Yes. The only way this would have changed would have been for one of them to embrace sin so much that he rejected God's promises—and thus jumped ship.

By the way, when you sit in a pew at church, you're sitting in the part of the room called the *nave*. It's the same word from which we get *navy*, from the Latin word for *boat*. By His grace, Jesus has brought you into the ark of His Church, and He's promised to deliver you to heaven. So confess your sins and stay at home with your Savior. And if you've run away for a while, rejoice that He remains faithful and rejoices to bring you back inside (Luke 15:10–24).

My faith feels really weak. What do i do?

First off, let that feeling of weakness be a reminder of how much you need the Lord's grace and help. People who believe they're strong often start to think they don't need a Savior.

More important, feed your faith! If your body is weak, you want to get food. If your faith feels weak, feed on God's Word. If you are properly prepared, go and receive the Lord's Supper. Confess your sins, including those that have made your faith weak (neglecting God's Word, filling your mind with worldly junk, etc.), and rejoice that you're forgiven. Faith is strengthened by forgiveness.

How weak can faith be before it's not faith anymore?

Faith ceases to be faith when it no longer clings to Jesus and forgiveness. Unless someone has publicly renounced the faith or is living obviously contrary to Scripture, you and I can't judge when someone has completely lost faith. What, for instance, about people who only come to church on Christmas and Easter? Do they have faith? I don't know. I know that if they do, they're not feeding it much. My point is this: always resist the temptation to wonder how much you can sin before you've really put your faith in danger. If you give in, there's a good chance you'll wander away from the faith without even realizing. Instead, rejoice that God gives you His Word, feed on it, and strengthen your faith daily!

You said faith clings to Jesus and forgiveness. Doesn't it enable us to do good things too?

107

Yes. We'll talk about this in section 4.

What would you call faith— is it a virtue? a skill? a talent? a behavior?

I'm not sure you can classify faith as anything but what the Bible calls it, a "gift of God" (Ephesians 2:8). But to get a better grasp of what faith is, we should also examine what faith isn't. That's the topic of the next chapter.

Section Three:
What Faith Isn't

108   I'll be honest with you, it's tough to explain
what faith is. It's a gift of God quite unlike any
other gift—it doesn't have a parallel in this
world that I can find, and I'm thinking a funnel
with hands may not do it complete justice. So
to help us understand what faith is, we need
to spend a few pages talking about what faith
isn't; and to help us understand what faith
does, we also need to know what it doesn't do.

1. Faith does not cling to the entire Bible.

The first time I heard this, I had a hard
time with it. If the entire Bible is God's Word,

shouldn't we believe in all of it? The answer is yes, since all of it is God's Word. But that's not what it means to say that faith doesn't cling to the entire Bible.

Remember, what does faith do? It holds on to Jesus and His promises of forgiveness, right? Faith is all about getting forgiveness, life, and salvation for you—and these are all gifts because Jesus has done all the work. All faith is interested in is life in Christ for you. Therefore, faith doesn't hold on to whatever doesn't give life. It's very narrow-minded that way.

God's Law is good and right and holy, but it doesn't give life. Quite the opposite! God's Law shows you how dead in sin you truly are. That's necessary for you to know, but knowing you're dead isn't the same as being alive. Faith clings to life, so it doesn't cling to the Law. That's why the Bible says,

109

> For we hold that one is justified by faith apart from works of the law. **(Romans 3:28)**

> Yet we know that a person is not justified by works of the law but through faith in Jesus Christ, so we also have believed in Christ Jesus, in order to be justified by faith in Christ and not by works of the law, because by works

of the law no one will be justified.
(Galatians 2:16)

Faith doesn't cling to the Law, and this is a very good thing for you. Faith says, "I know I'm saved because Jesus died and rose for me—He got the job done!" If faith clings to the Law, too, then it would say, "I know I'm saved because Jesus died and rose for me, and because I keep God's commandments well enough." So here's the question: how well would you have to keep God's commandments to keep them "enough"? You'd have to keep them perfectly, because one little sin makes you completely sinful (James 2:10)! That's why you're quite happy your salvation is built on Jesus only, and that's what faith grabs with an iron grip.

Back in section 1, we used the illustration of Deadguy, a man with no heartbeat in the emergency room. The first thing the doctors would do is determine that he's dead. They can even tell the man he's dead—but that doesn't help him at all. What helps him is when the doctors restore his heartbeat and bring him back to life. Faith is all about life. The Law tells you that you're dead, but knowing you're dead doesn't make you alive. Jesus and His forgiveness make you alive, and that's what faith holds on to.

Likewise, faith doesn't hold on to the history

110

of the Bible. The Bible contains a lot of history, starting with the creation of the heavens and the earth. It tells about the flood and ancient history of the Middle East, and it also gives us the historical accounts of Jesus' life on earth from His birth to His ascension. The Bible is full of history, and it's full of examples of how God miraculously intervened in history for us; and because of those miracles, many doubt that the history in the Bible is accurate. By faith, we believe it's all true—and yet, faith doesn't cling to history.

You're not saved because you accept that God created the heavens and the earth in six days, or because you believe the walls of **111** Jericho fell down. Those are both true, but they don't give forgiveness—and faith only holds on to what saves you. In fact, you're not saved by believing that Jesus was born, or that He lived, or that He died. You're saved by believing that He died on the cross to save you from sin.

Which brings us to our next point . . .

2. Faith isn't a group thing. it's personal.

Every individual Christian has faith. In other words, faith says, "I myself am saved because I trust that Jesus died for me." Sounds obvious, right?

Not so much, actually. I've run into too many people who say, "I am a Christian because I belong to a church. I don't go, but I belong." Their argument boils down to this: "I must have faith because I belong to a place where other people have faith." Variations include, "I am a Christian because I come from a Christian family," or "I live in a country that's been described as a 'Christian nation,' therefore I am a Christian." A frightening version is, "I'm a Christian because I go to church."

112 This is the same argument as "I must be in great shape because I belong to a health club. I don't go, but I belong." (It is not the same argument as "Since I go to the grocery store, I am an avocado," as one would certainly be more likely to become an eggplant instead.) It simply doesn't work that way. Faith is personal—it is what connects you personally to Jesus and His forgiveness.

As Jesus proclaimed the Gospel on the way to the cross, His fellow Jews sometimes objected, "Abraham is our father" (John 8:39; see also verse 53). In other words, "We are God's people because of our family line; we don't need to believe in You." Jesus' response is big.

> Jesus said to them, "If you were
> Abraham's children, you would be

> doing the works Abraham did, but
> now you seek to kill Me, a man who
> has told you the truth that I heard
> from God. This is not what Abraham
> did." **(John 8:39–40)**

For one thing, Abraham wasn't saved because he was Abraham. He was saved because he trusted in God (Romans 4:3). He was saved by faith. If Abraham was saved by faith, why wouldn't his descendants be saved the same way? Look at the other thing Jesus pointed out: while His listeners claimed to be following God apart from Him, they were plotting to kill Him! In fact, when the chief priests eventually arranged His crucifixion, they believed it was a great service to God. However, whoever rejects the Son of God also rejects the Father, because they are one in the Holy Trinity.

This is an important lesson about faith: if you believe you're saved by something apart from Jesus—your own good behavior or your membership in a church—then what you believe is harmful. It says you're not saved by Jesus—it rejects the only Savior.

With that, we'd better move on to the next point, namely that . . .

3. Faith isn't personal. it's a group thing.

Huh? But isn't this the opposite of number two? Not really. What I mean is this: we live in an age where it's trendy to personalize everything—cars, computers, stuffed bears, and so forth. It's very tempting for people to treat faith the same way, like someone saying, "I believe in Jesus, but my Jesus says I don't need to go to church." It's pretty common for people to think they can personalize their faith however they like, and whatever they come up with is true and God-pleasing.

But that's wrong! Saving faith is the same for everyone; it's what holds on to Jesus and His forgiveness for you. It clings to His person and work—who He is and what He does—as revealed in the Bible. In that sense, you have the same faith as Abraham, St. Paul, and every other Christian, because all Christians are saved by the forgiveness Jesus has won.

Which sets us up nicely for number four . . .

4. Faith doesn't trust a fake or modified Jesus.

A lot of people who believe they believe in Jesus really don't believe in Him. Why? Because they've created an imaginary Jesus to believe in.

Imagine a man who has to take medicine

for some condition. We'll call the medicine Yucktiva. The pills are small, round, and white. They work—they treat the condition—but they also have some really bad side effects, and he feels crummy all the time. The man comes up with a solution. He buys some mints that are about the same size and shape, and says, "From now on, I shall call these mints 'Yucktiva.' I shall believe they are truly the medicine I must have. Because I take them regularly, I will be healthy. I will feel better too. Furthermore, I will even have fresh breath with hints of peppermint and wintergreen." The man is partially correct; for the time being, he will indeed have fresh breath with hints of peppermint and wintergreen. However, he becomes sick and grows only more and more ill. "But how can this be?" he wonders. "I'm still taking my medicine, just like I was supposed to."

115

You, of course, know exactly what's wrong. Just because he renamed the mints doesn't mean they've become medicine. He is probably not in the running for any Genius of the 21st Century awards.

But here's a question to ponder: what does the man trust for healing in the first place? If you said he trusts the mints, I don't think that's quite right. Actually, he trusts himself. He's convinced that all he has to do is believe that candy becomes medicine and it does! What incredible telekinetic powers he must have! But if that's the case, why couldn't he just believe the disease right out of himself in the first place?

Foolish, right? Unfortunately, though, people do this with Jesus all the time. Sadly, I hear too many people say, "I believe in Jesus, that He was a great man and a great teacher who lived and died—but He wasn't the Son of God or anything like that." Or, "I believe Jesus is the Son of God, but I don't believe He's going to condemn people for sin." Or, "I believe Jesus is the Savior, but not the only one; you can get to heaven by following different paths of different religions." When people say these things, they're not talking about Jesus, the Son of God who was born of Mary, who died and rose again for you. They've created a different, imaginary Jesus to trust in.

But here's the thing, they don't really trust in that imaginary Jesus. They're trusting themselves for eternal life, since they're the ones who made up the fake savior. That isn't saving faith. Instead, it's trusting in yourself to raise you from the dead.

Faith clings to the Gospel because the Gospel proclaims the real Jesus. It proclaims who He is and what He has done. Faith doesn't pick parts of Jesus to believe in and reject others. It embraces the whole Savior who has died for the sins of the world.

5. Faith isn't knowledge.
Or is it?

You're not saved by knowing who Jesus is. Even the demons knew that Jesus is the Messiah (Mark 1:24), but that didn't save them. A lot of people know what the Bible says about Jesus—they simply don't believe it's true. In that sense, faith isn't knowledge. You're not saved by knowing about Jesus. You're saved by believing in Him.

117

On the other hand, knowledge is part of faith. As you hear God's Word, and the Holy Spirit works faith in you, you also gain knowledge. You know what you believe in. You couldn't say, "I believe in Jesus, but I have no idea what that means."

You're not saved because you know who Jesus is; but you know who Jesus is because you've heard the Word and believe.

6. Faith isn't acceptance.
Or is it?

This is a good test question from what you've read so far. It's a matter of how you define *acceptance*.

People confuse faith with agreeing to a logical argument. For instance, when discussing the resurrection, it's a very good thing to point out the missing body. If Jesus didn't rise from the dead, what happened to His body? If it was truly stolen by the disciples (Matthew 28:13), why wasn't there a massive manhunt to track them down for violating Roman law? And why would the disciples devote their lives—and suffer death—to proclaim a story they knew wasn't true?

118 If you ask me, those are pretty good questions to ask. You might even find someone saying, "You know what? That makes sense. Because that makes sense to me, I accept that Jesus rose from the dead." That's fine—but it's not faith. Faith doesn't accept Jesus because your mind has decided it makes sense. Faith trusts because the Word proclaims Jesus.

On the other hand, it's absolutely true that faith accepts the forgiveness and life Jesus gives in His Word. But it's not your mind making the conscious decision to accept Jesus; instead, it's faith—that gift and work of the Holy Spirit—grabbing on to grace for you.

7. Faith is not a tattoo.

A tattoo is just a mark on the skin and nothing more. It marks you, but it's just something that happened one time. For instance, a gang member might get a tattoo to show he's a part of the gang. He might leave the lifestyle behind and start all over again; but even though he's changed, he still has the tattoo. It's outdated—it doesn't correctly identify him anymore.

People have been known to treat faith like a tattoo. Some believe that you're saved if God chose you and lost if God has chosen to damn you. (Remember Calvin in section 1?) In that case, you're saved if God "marked" you to be saved, not because you have faith that clings to Jesus. Another example of this would be the unrepentant sinner who says, "Even though I don't care about breaking God's laws every day of my life, I know I'm going to heaven because I was baptized as a baby."

119

This is as brilliant as saying, "My dog must still be alive because I saw him breathing twenty-five years ago." Sorry, but Fido still has to be breathing right now to be alive right now. Faith is the same way—it's not something that happened once upon a time and marked you for life. It's the ongoing grasping of Jesus and His forgiveness.

8. Faith is not the same as good behavior.

A lot of people think Christianity is all about good behavior or moral living; someone leads a Christian life when she's friendly and kind and does nice things for other people. Now as Christians, we certainly ought to be serving those around us, since we're commanded to "love your neighbor as yourself" (Romans 13:9). But loving and other good works aren't faith. Faith is all about holding on to the Gospel, while good works are all about obeying the Law. Faith is about clinging to life in Christ, while good works are what we do after we've been made alive.

120

Quickly, jump back to the example of Deadguy in the ER, his heart stopped. He's not going to become alive if he treats his wife well and takes care of his kids. He can't do those things because he's dead. However, once he's been made alive, he can get back to doing those things. Faith makes you alive; once you're alive, then you can do good things because of faith.

There's another way faith can be misunderstood: it can be tempting for us to believe that people—ourselves included—are closer to God when our behavior looks good to us and those around us. But remember the Pharisees—the "white-washed tombs"—they looked great on the outside, but inside they were dead. On the other hand, no one considered tax collectors and prostitutes to be moral at all; but Jesus told the Pharisees:

> Truly, I say to you, the tax collectors and the prostitutes go into the kingdom of God before you. For John came to you in the way of righteousness, and you did not believe him, but the tax collectors and the prostitutes believed him. And even when you saw it, you did not afterward change your minds and believe him.
> (Matthew 21:31–32)

121

Jesus told the Pharisees that prostitutes were more likely to get into heaven than they were! Why? Because the Pharisees believed they were saved by their works—that's not faith, because it doesn't hold on to Jesus and His works. Repentant prostitutes, on the other hand, didn't trust in their moral acts—they had none; thus, when they heard God's Word, they trusted in Jesus to save them. That's faith at work.

9. Faith does not come through anything but the Word of God.

We already looked at Romans 10:17: "So faith comes from hearing, and hearing through the word of Christ." God promises to give faith by His Word. Now back up to verse 14: "How then will they call on Him in whom they have not believed? And how are they to believe in Him of whom they have never heard? And how are they to hear without someone preaching?" God doesn't promise to give faith apart from His Word.

This means faith doesn't come through works. We just said it's not the same as good behavior, so now we'll add that it doesn't come from good behavior. In other words, you can't say, "I believe in Jesus because I've done enough to serve Him." This isn't like earning a bonus at an after-school job, where you get a gift certificate for working hard. Faith is a gift, right? Therefore, it's not something you earn from your works.

This also means faith doesn't come from experiences, emotional highs, encounters with nature, or anything else. Some will say they believe in Jesus because they narrowly escaped death in an accident; but believing that Jesus saved you from a car wreck is not the same as

122

believing He died on the cross to take away your sins. Only the second one is faith because only the second one is holding on to Jesus for forgiveness. Likewise, there are plenty of people who will tell you they "feel close to God" when they're alone in the forest or sitting on a mountain. Frankly, I enjoy those things too, and I often marvel at the Creator's creativity. It does good things for my mental and emotional health. But trees and mountains don't give forgiveness or faith—feeling close to God because you're excited about nature doesn't save you.

The comfort here is that faith is far more constant than emotions, which come and go. You'll feel different from Sunday to Sunday as you go to church, perhaps because of your health or how much sleep you had or how much of a pain your little brother was at the breakfast table. But no matter your emotional state, Jesus still offers forgiveness in His means of grace, and faith still clings to Him.

123

10. Faith does not make you bulletproof.

It can be easy to believe a Christian should have a better life than a non-Christian—after all, you have faith in Jesus, right? Therefore, God should be looking out for you. Rest assured,

God is looking out for you—if He weren't, Jesus wouldn't have died for you. But remember: faith clings to Jesus, right? Therefore, it doesn't contradict Jesus or say things He doesn't say. One of the things Jesus says is, "In the world you will have tribulation. But take heart; I have overcome the world" (John 16:33). As long as we live in this sinful world, we're going to face trouble and suffering—just as Jesus did. But take heart: He overcame the world for you and rose again from the dead. Therefore, on the Last Day, He's going to deliver you from all trouble too. In the meantime, He allows trouble in your life—but only for your ultimate good. We'll talk more about this in the chapters on prayer and miracles.

In the meantime, though, don't buy into the false belief that faith makes you bulletproof. The devil loves it if you do—because then when you get hit with trouble, you're likely to conclude that God's a liar or that you don't have faith. The textbook illustration is Job. In His wisdom (which I don't pretend to understand), God allowed the devil to afflict Job terribly so Job lost his family, goods, and health in a very short time. What was Job's response? "The Lord gave, and the Lord has taken away; blessed be the name of the Lord" (Job 1:21). That's a confession of faith! Despite what Job saw and suffered, he still trusted the Lord. Furthermore, it was faith in Jesus. Later on, as trouble continued, he confessed:

> For I know that my Redeemer lives, and at the last He will stand upon the earth. And after my skin has been thus destroyed, yet in my flesh I shall see God, whom I shall see for myself, and my eyes shall behold, and not another. (Job 19:25–27)

Job knew he wasn't bulletproof in a sinful world. But he trusted God would deliver him for Jesus' sake. That's what faith does.

Faith isn't any of these things. It can't be, because of what it is—a gift of God that holds on to Jesus for you, given through His Word. Since that's the case, faith can't be something you do by your own reason or strength—especially since you're dead in sin without faith.

So faith can't cling to the entire Bible. If it did, you'd have to say, "I'm saved in part by keeping the Law." But you're not saved by your works—so faith doesn't cling to the Law.

Faith isn't yours because you belong to a group. If it was, you'd be saved by your work of joining a church, not by the forgiveness Jesus has won.

Faith can't be a personal thing, where you decide what to believe about Jesus. If it were,

125

you'd be saved by what you chose to believe, not by what Jesus has done.

Likewise, faith doesn't trust a fake or modified Jesus. If it did, you'd be saved by the savior you worked to create with your sinful mind, not by the One who died on the cross for you.

Faith isn't knowledge. If it were, you'd be saved by how much you've worked to learn, not by Jesus' death for you.

Faith isn't acceptance. If it were, you'd be saved by how well you work at thinking, not by Jesus' cross.

126 Faith isn't a tattoo. If it were, you'd be saved because you just happened to be picked by God, not because faith holds on to Jesus.

Faith isn't the same as good behavior. If it were, you'd be saved by keeping rules—and you'd be lost if you sinned too much. That's how the Law works—not the Gospel.

Faith doesn't come through anything but the Word of God. If it came through your emotions or experiences, you'd be saved by what you feel or what you do.

Whenever someone says something about faith, run it through the filter:

> * If it's not a gift, it's not faith.
>
> * If it doesn't hold on to Jesus, it's not faith.

* If it's something you do,
  it's not faith.

* If it comes through something
  besides His Word, it's not faith.

Faith is far better than that. It's God's gift that holds on to Jesus for you, so you can have eternal life. Luther's Small Catechism sums it up in the explanation to the Third Article of the Apostles' Creed. I hope you'll forgive me for a few bracketed comments, but I'm always amazed at how much good stuff Dr. Luther could squeeze into a few short sentences:

> I [faith is personal] believe that I cannot by my own reason [faith isn't my knowledge] or strength [faith isn't my works or good behavior] believe in Jesus Christ, my Lord, or come to Him; but the Holy Spirit [faith is the work of the Holy Spirit] has called me [it's not me accepting by my strength, but receiving His gift] by the Gospel [faith comes by hearing the Word], enlightened me with His gifts [it's a gift, not something I do], sanctified and kept me [faith isn't a one-time tattoo] in the true faith [faith clings only to Jesus and forgiveness, nothing else].
>
> In the same way He calls, gathers, enlightens, and sanctifies the whole Christian Church on earth [faith is a group thing], and keeps it with Jesus

127

Christ in the one true faith.

In this Christian church He daily and richly forgives all my sins and the sins of all believers [and with forgiveness comes faith].

On the Last Day He will raise me and all the dead [you're not bulletproof now . . .], and give eternal life to me and all believers in Christ [. . . but you will be!].

This is most certainly true.
(SC, p. 17)

Look how that starts out! "I believe . . . that I cannot believe . . . but the Holy Spirit has called me by the Gospel."

There you go.

Any questions?

128

Q&A:
You Ask . . .

if someone is really sorry for his sins, is he saved?

No. Being sorry is not the same as trusting in Jesus. The poster child is Judas, who deeply regretted that he'd betrayed Jesus—but didn't trust in Him for forgiveness (Matthew 27:3–4). Think of it this way: if you were saved for being really sorry, it would mean you were saved by your work of being sorry enough. If that were true, you'd no longer be saved by Jesus and His forgiveness alone.

Repentance has two parts—sorrow for sin (also known as *contrition*) and trust in Jesus and forgiveness (also known as *faith*). Contrition prepares you for forgiveness, since the one who isn't sorry doesn't want to be forgiven; but only faith saves.

You said faith doesn't cling to the Law, because the Law doesn't save us. So can we just ignore the Law?

No! God's Law is holy and serves a definite purpose: it shows us our sin (Romans 3:20; 7:7). It shows us our need for Jesus and forgiveness. If we didn't know we were sinful, how would we know our need to be saved? Thus Romans 3:31 declares, "Do we then overthrow the law by this faith? By no means! On the contrary, we uphold the law."

The Law doesn't save us, so faith doesn't cling to it; but the Law shows us our need for the Savior that faith does cling to.

if faith clings only to Jesus and forgiveness, and not to the history in the Bible, how can you say "i believe the history in the Bible is true"?

130

Good question. As we talk about faith in this book, we're talking about *saving* faith. *Faith* can be used in other senses, but in the New Testament it is almost exclusively a reference to faith in Jesus. I can believe other things. I believe, for instance, that God created the heavens and the earth in six 24-hour days and rested on the seventh. In other words, I believe the story of creation in Genesis 1 is historically accurate and true. However, that isn't saving faith because believing in a six-day creation doesn't get me forgiven.

You said above that faith is personal. When I started talking about "my personal faith," my pastor twitched. Did this send up some sort of warning flag?

Maybe. One of the biggest headaches we pastors encounter is that people mix up the ideas of personal faith and group faith. (Look back at points two and three at the beginning of this chapter.) Remember, faith is personal because God gives it to you personally. But faith is a "group thing" in that God gives the same faith (both faith and the faith) to all.

We live in a world of choices. If I buy a computer or a car or an ice cream cone, I can make a bunch of choices to personalize it just the way I want it. That's okay. But people want to treat the faith the same way. Many treat the Christian faith as if it were the basic model of a car. It's nice and all, but now you've got to put your own stuff on it in order to make it your own. That's when the idea of "personal faith" gets abused. Instead of saying, "God has given faith to me personally so I can believe the faith," people say, "God has given the faith and I've done some picking and choosing with it. I personally believe this part and personally don't believe that part." Examples could include: "The Bible says living together without marriage is wrong in general, but it's okay for me personally;" or "The bulletin at this church says I should talk to the pastor before I commune, but I don't believe I have to." It's wrong, not to mention rude, to say, "I'm going to insist on my way, because of what I personally believe."

Now, I'm not accusing you of doing this—I don't know enough about the situation. But that could be why your pastor twitched. Depending on the day, I might have blinked hard too. But each of us needs to be sure what we personally believe is the same faith God gives for all people. Whenever we modify it to suit ourselves, we're not adding something good—we're taking away from what's true.

My friend is not a Christian, and we debate religion a lot. My arguments about why Christianity is true make a lot of sense, and he even admits that his don't. Why won't he believe?

I can't answer that question, but let me offer this. First off, good for you that you're talking about religion with a friend who needs to hear about Jesus; I wish more people would. Don't be discouraged, but remember this: arguments— even the best, outstanding arguments—don't give faith. Only the Gospel does. I don't know what you've been debating, it might be creation vs. evolution, evidence for the flood, or all sorts of things. But while these debates can show your friend that his position is weak, they don't give him forgiveness. No forgiveness means no faith, since the two go together.

133

Hey, keep debating! And as you do, work Jesus into the conversation. Tell about His death on the cross. If you're talking creation, then talk about how He makes you a new creation by grace (2 Corinthians 5:17). If you're talking about the flood, talk about how Jesus has washed away your sins in Baptism (1 Peter 3:20–21). Talk about the Gospel! Will your friend believe? I don't know. The Holy Spirit works when and where He wills—but He wills to work through the Gospel.

Do i believe in the Bible because i believe in Jesus, or vice versa?

This is a really important question for evangelism. What does faith cling to? It clings to Jesus, not all of the Bible, right? Therefore, you and I believe the Bible is true because we first believe in Jesus. Faith in the Savior leads to trust in His Word.

Sometimes, people mistakenly think we need to believe the Bible is God's Word before we can believe in Jesus, so they try to evangelize by convincing people God's Word is true. Don't get me wrong, I'm all for presenting evidence that God's Word is true (this is called *apologetics*), because you can refute a lot of "proofs" against the Bible. However, faith clings to Jesus, not to evidence that Jericho really existed. When you evangelize, speak the Evangel—speak the Gospel.

Can infants have faith?

Yes. Faith is a gift from God with no requirements from us. Why couldn't an infant believe? What would prevent an infant from believing if

134

God gives Him forgiveness in Holy Baptism?

Well, you said faith includes knowledge, acceptance, and trust. How can a baby have these things?

Because God gives them to babies with forgiveness. Give babies credit for knowing a little, anyway. When infants are born, they need food. Where do they get it? They nurse from their mothers. Why? Because they know enough to know that milk is food. They accept and trust that the milk is for them. They don't understand the nutritional properties of milk or exactly who mom is, but they know God has provided food for them there. Call it instinct if you want—it's still God-given knowledge. When it comes to faith, who knows how much baptized infants know about God? On the other hand, we know this for sure—God gives forgiveness in Holy Baptism, and faith comes with forgiveness. We'll talk more about this in Chapter 5.

135

My grandma has Alzheimer's disease really bad. She's been a Christian all her life, but now she doesn't remember anything. Does she still have faith?

It's really, really tough to watch someone deteriorate with Alzheimer's disease, and you have my sympathy. This is a situation where I'm especially thankful that faith is a gift of God, not something we have to come up with or maintain. As far as faith goes, I treat patients with Alzheimer's disease much the same way as I treat a very small child. Where a patient confessed the faith before dementia set in, I speak God's Word to her with the confidence that God is still preserving her with forgiveness and faith. If I visit a patient with Alzheimer's disease who has never been a Christian, I still speak God's Word to him with the prayer that the Lord might still give him faith as his life draws to a close. Sometimes, because of dementia, a Christian will start to say the most ungodly things because of past mistakes; but Jesus has died for those sins, as well.

Jesus is faithful to your grandma: when she was baptized, He promised to be with her always. I give thanks that, if I should suffer in the same way and even forget my own name, Jesus will remember it. He's written it in His book of life (Revelation 21:27).

You warned against saying, "i'm a Christian because i go to church."

you ask about . . . FAiTH

What did you mean?

You and I will always be tempted to say, "God loves me because of what I do, not because of what Jesus has done." That temptation just goes with being sinful. So it's possible to for someone to say, "God loves me because I've done the good work of going to church and sitting through the sermon." But God doesn't call us to worship so we can earn points by our behavior. God calls us to worship because that's where we hear His Word—and it's in His Word that He gives us forgiveness.

Faith comes from hearing God's Word. **137** What if i tell someone what the Bible says without quoting it exactly?

Jesus is called the Word in John 1:1. If you've told them accurately what the Bible says about Jesus, you've proclaimed the Word to them.

This question sounds stupid, but i'll ask it anyway. if faith comes by hearing, can deaf people be saved?

It's actually not a bad question, because it

helps us clarify a little bit more. First, Jesus died for all—therefore all people, no matter their disabilities, can be saved. Second, the Word of God can still work when recipients don't hear. Lazarus wasn't actively listening when Jesus told him to come out of the tomb (John 11:43), because he was dead. I mention this because in the case of the Baptism of a deaf baby, God still gets the job done whether or not the baby hears.

I'm not saying, however, that we should just speak the Word to deaf adults who can't hear what we're saying. Whether or not God's Word works on its own, they—like us—are being bombarded with temptations and information designed to make them reject the faith. Therefore, we want to communicate the faith in ways they can understand—such as print or sign language. Is it possible to hear without ears? I would say yes! In Numbers 12:6, God declared that He would speak with prophets in dreams. Dreams are internal, yes? When you hear things in dreams, you hear them without your ears. I would say as the deaf receive God's Word through print or sign language, they're receiving it and God is giving faith.

Can God give faith apart from His Word?

you ask about . . . FAITH

God can do whatever He wants to. However, He's promised to give forgiveness and faith by means of His Word, including His Word in Holy Baptism and Holy Communion. He doesn't promise you'll find forgiveness anywhere else. So why would anyone look for forgiveness where God hasn't promised it, while neglecting where He has?

So can i "hear" the Word by reading the Bible at home? if so, why should i go listen to a pastor?

When you read the Bible on your own, it's still God's Word and the Holy Spirit is at work. Pretty cool, huh? However, I think you want to be careful not to use that good truth in order to justify bad behavior. When the Bible says that "faith comes from hearing" (Romans 10:17), the context is the proclamation that God sends out preachers to proclaim His Word—He desires that we hear the Word from those whom He has called. Why? In part, because it reminds us that our "personal faith" isn't something we construct on our own, but it's given to us by God. It comes into us from outside us. At any rate, the Lord makes clear that we are to gather together (Hebrews 10:25) to hear His Word and receive His Sacraments.

Why does my pastor have to be so boring when he preaches a sermon?

Well. Hmm . . . you understand I have a bias here. You do, too, so let's set those aside.

We live in a time where advertisers know they have about fifteen seconds to grab you; commercials are all about entertainment, to get your attention on their product. This mentality has invaded the Church. For instance, people don't read the Bible because it's not as "user friendly" as a novel. To address your question, others maintain that the pastor has to be an engaging speaker in order to "sell" the Gospel. It might be good for advertising, but it's not good theology. In his first letter to the church at Corinth, Paul wrote, "For Christ did not send me to baptize but to preach the gospel, and not with words of eloquent wisdom, lest the cross of Christ be emptied of its power" (1 Corinthians 1:17). Paul didn't rely on eloquent speaking; in fact, he was wary of slick preachers. Jesus' bloody cross didn't look very attractive, but that's where salvation was won. Even if Paul's preaching of the cross wasn't eloquent, Jesus still gave salvation.

What gives you faith? God's Word does! Dynamic speaking doesn't. If your pastor is an engaging speaker, that's nice; but if he's not preaching God's Word, your faith isn't getting strengthened no matter how much you enjoy his speech. If you find your pastor to be boring, it may be that he's not a great speaker; but if he's correctly preaching God's Word, your sins are being forgiven and your faith is getting fed. So repent. Rather than use your pastor's speaking style as an excuse to ignore the Gospel, rejoice that God has given you someone who will strengthen your faith by telling you God's Word. And, set free from the sin of finding fault with others, maybe work on your listening skills a little too.

Two more thoughts: as a pastor, I'd rather sound interesting than boring, but neither one gives you faith. God's Word does. I'd also rather have a competent brain surgeon who bores me than an incompetent one who tells good jokes. A lot of things are more important than entertainment.

How should i feel during worship?

This kind of goes with the previous question, and it's important to remember that faith and emotions are not the same thing. This is good because whether you feel up or down, Jesus doesn't change but remains faithful to you.

Anyway, there's a big argument these days that worship should be designed to be emotionally engaging, even entertaining. I think that's barking up the wrong tree. As we'll see in section 5, worship is about receiving the forgiveness of sins and getting your faith strengthened—no matter how you feel.

Look, I've been at worship services that left me feeling like they'd dragged on forever, and I've been at worship services that I didn't want to end. Sometimes it's because the service went well, or because of good or bad news outside of worship; sometimes, it's because I had a good or bad night of sleep. My emotions are going to change from hour to hour, so I'll feel different about worship.

So how should we feel? Thankful! Thankful that no matter how we feel, the Lord still comes in His means of grace to give us forgiveness and strengthen our faith.

My friend said his church teaches that creeds are "dead"—they're just statements on paper, and what matters is what we believe. How should i respond?

In the Lutheran Church, we make use of three creeds: the Apostles' Creed, the Nicene

Creed, and the Athanasian Creed. All three of these are statements which sum up the Christian faith. Because they sum up the faith, they're not dead or outdated. They're valuable summaries of what the Bible says.

It's true that we're saved by faith, not by having creeds on paper. But if a creed correctly reflects God's Word, shouldn't we believe what it says—shouldn't our faith be in the faith? And why would it be wrong to use the same words to repeat the same truths? The answer is often, "Because the words lose their meaning," but that's incorrect. The words keep their meaning, but we sinners stop paying attention. That's not the creeds' fault, but ours.

143

When people tell me that these creeds are old or dead, I show them what the creeds say and ask which part they disagree with. Usually, they find nothing to disagree with. If they do, then we'll go take a look at what the Bible says.

You talked about how people can create a false Jesus and not even know it. How much about Jesus can you get wrong before you've created a false savior?

I don't know that we can answer that. Certainly you've gone off track if you deny that Jesus is both God and man, or that He died for your sins and rose again. All other errors are looking to undermine those truths. But before you get there, how much can you get wrong? I don't think we can pinpoint an answer. But we do know this: Jesus tells you all you need to know about Him in His Word, so keep learning! The more truth you know, the less susceptible you are to error.

Now i'm worried. To be a Christian, i have to believe in Jesus. What if i misunderstand something, or get a teaching or two wrong? What do i have to believe to be a Christian, and how much can i get wrong before i'm not?

This is a great question and a very important one. It's also a tricky one to answer. Clearly, Christians don't walk in lockstep in beliefs these days, a situation that should grieve us all. Why do Christians disagree? In large part, it is because they use different rules for interpreting the Bible. At any rate, it's the situation in which we find ourselves.

To put my cards on the table, I'm a Lutheran,

and the rules I've listed in the introduction are a summary of how we Lutherans have historically interpreted the Bible. It's the best way, because it lets the Bible speak for itself. The reason I bring it up is that we conservative Lutherans tend to be pretty persnickety about what we teach and believe. We're not willing to say, "Since other Christians disagree with this or that teaching, let's just give it up in order to get along more." We don't do this to be mean, we do it because we want to hold on to all of God's Word. We want to conserve it, which is what it should mean to be *conservative*, so we still have it all to proclaim to generations yet unborn (see Psalm 78:5–7).

The reason I bring this up now is we tend to rankle other Christians with our care of Scripture, and some get a little mad and respond, "You Lutherans believe you're the only ones going to heaven!" I'm quite happy to tell them we don't believe that. In fact, we explicitly condemn such a notion as a false teaching.

Here's the deal: to be a Christian is to believe in Jesus. As Paul and Silas said to the jailer in Acts 16:31, "Believe in the Lord Jesus, and you will be saved, you and your household." You need to know who Jesus is—the eternal Son of God, and Second Person of the Trinity, who

145

became flesh and was born of Mary. If you don't know who Jesus is, you could be believing in a different god that you've named "Jesus."

Furthermore, you need to know what He's done for you—namely, that He's died on the cross to take away your sins and risen again. If you don't know that, you can't trust that you're forgiven. But to believe in who Jesus is and what He's done is to be forgiven (Romans 10:9).

The person and work of Jesus is the Gospel. The Bible teaches all sorts of other things too; and we're supposed to follow them as well. You're probably not going to get them all right. I'm going to mess up too. That's why we rejoice to confess all of our sins—even the ones we don't know (Psalm 19:12). This includes the false teachings we ignorantly believe. But because we believe in Jesus, we're forgiven for those sins and remain Christians. And when we become aware of a false teaching we've clung to ignorantly, we repent of it and cling to the truth. Why wouldn't we?

Okay, so does that mean once i believe in Jesus, i don't have to worry about what the rest of the Bible says?

No! Your sinful flesh would love that. It sure isn't the response of a Christian. The Christian delights in God's Word and meditates on it day and night (Psalm 1:1–2).

For one thing, God gives you His entire Word as His gift to you. Why would you snatch just one part—admittedly the life-giving part— and not care about the rest? All of Scripture points to Jesus and His salvation for you, and it's given to strengthen your faith. Why would you leave your faith weak?

Likewise, the more you study the Scriptures, the more of God's Word you're going to know. The more truth you're going to have. More truth means less error. More truth means stronger faith. More error means less truth. More error means weaker faith and a greater chance of giving in to temptation and rejecting Jesus.

Your old sinful flesh wants you to have the least amount of biblical knowledge possible, since that will make it easier to snatch you away from Jesus.

You said that believing Jesus was born, lived, and died wasn't faith. i thought Jesus' death on the cross was the Gospel. Could you explain?

You don't need faith to believe that Jesus was born, lived, or died. That happens to everybody. The Gospel isn't just that Jesus died, but that Jesus died and rose again for you—to take away your sins. That's the part you can only believe by faith.

Sometimes people talk about blind faith. is faith blind?

It all depends on what you mean. Hebrews 11:1 says, "Now faith is the assurance of things hoped for, the conviction of things not seen." Faith trusts in what you can't see, like forgiveness, Jesus, eternal life, and so forth. Someone might use *blind faith* to describe this. In that case, we rejoice that though faith might be blind, it's not deaf—it always hears and clings to the Gospel.

On the other hand, *blind faith* sometimes means "unquestioning faith," as in "I'll just go ahead and believe what the pastor says without checking it against God's Word," or "This church must be teaching the truth because of what it says on the sign outside." This is a bad idea. You should always check a pastor's sermon or a church's teachings (or this book) against God's Word.

Can a soldier who is a Christian expect extra protection from death?

Remember, faith doesn't make you bullet-proof—in this case, literally. We Christians should not be surprised when we suffer in this world, though that suffering may come in all sorts of ways. Faith clings to Jesus and the forgiveness of sins so we can be confident of "the resurrection of the dead and the life of the world to come" (Nicene Creed, *LSB*, p. 158). That way, we're prepared for death whenever it might come. Our time is in God's hands.

Section Four: Faith and Good Works

By now, I think we've made it pretty clear that we're saved solely by God's grace—we don't do anything to be saved. We can't—we're Deadguy. Therefore, if we're saved by faith, then faith isn't our work because we can't do it. Faith is a gift of God that holds on to Jesus. It's not our work.

Therefore, good works aren't necessary for salvation. This is a very good thing. If you had to do something—anything—to be saved, you could never be sure if you had done enough, well enough, to please God. If Jesus does it all, your salvation is absolutely certain, and that's something to rejoice in.

This completely free salvation for Jesus' sake, by the way, is the central teaching of Lutheran theology. It's not just "Lutheran" though; we've been demonstrating how it is most faithful to Scripture.

However, it's also the grounds for misunderstanding. Lutherans get accused a lot of saying that we Christians don't have to do good works. That certainly isn't what we say, because that would be a false teaching called *antinomianism*. (To impress your pastor, use that word in casual conversation. Try "Pastor, I'm glad that sermon had no antinomian tendencies." Or "I got a dog and named him Antinomianism.")

151

Here's the truth:

Good works are not necessary for salvation.

But good works are necessary.

I'm surprised how many people think it's a contradiction, because it's not a contradiction at all. To illustrate, we once again return to our beloved character, Deadguy. The day Deadguy ended up in the ER, he had a lot of things to do—good things. Some were about self-maintenance: eating meals, taking vitamins, and getting some exercise. He had other things to do for people around him: help customers at his job, stop by the store for his wife, play with his kids, and walk the dog. These are all good things to do.

However, Deadguy ended up in the ER with his heart stopped. When the doctors gathered around him, the conversation did not go like this:

> **Dr. A:** Look, it's Deadguy. He's dead.
>
> **Dr. B:** He sure is, and he can't do anything to save himself!
>
> **Dr. A:** That's for sure—taking vitamins or stopping by the store for his wife will not bring him back to life. They're not necessary to save him because they can't.
>
> **Dr. B:** Did you hear that, nurse? Dr. A just said Deadguy shouldn't ever take vitamins or stop by the store for his wife. That's just terrible! Don't you think he should help his wife?
>
> **Nurse:** Are you sure you two guys were smart enough to get through medical school?
>
> **Dr. A:** That's not what I said. I said helping his wife wouldn't get his heart going again.
>
> **Dr. B:** I can't believe you're so anti-family, Dr. A. You probably think he

shouldn't walk the dog either. Sure, dump that on his poor wife too. How could you?!

Dr. A: I didn't say that! What I meant was he can't help his wife because he's dead! We've got to make him alive again! Then he can help his wife!

Dr. B: What has that poor woman ever done to you? Why do you want to dump everything on her?

Dr. A: Stop squirting me with saline solution!

Dr. B: Only if you put down those forceps!

Dr. A: You first!

Dr. B: No, you!

Nurse: Oh, brother. Not again. I'll just go get Dr. C.

153

Get the idea? Dr. A has it right, except you should never point forceps at anyone unless it is absolutely necessary and you are trained to do so. Deadguy can't do any good works to save himself, because he's dead. However, once he's alive, he can—and should—do things like eat meals, walk the dog, and stop by the store for his wife. To say you have to do good works before you're alive is to put the cart before the horse. To say good works aren't necessary is to destroy the cart. And maybe squirt the horse with saline solution, but I'm not sure.

Anyway, Scripture teaches clearly that good works don't save us, because we're completely dead in sin. One verse that makes this crystal clear is Hebrews 11:6, "And without faith it is impossible to please [God]." Another is Romans 14:23: "For whatever does not proceed from faith is sin." Clearly, faith comes first, before good works.

But then good works follow! Forgiveness sets us free from sin. If we're set free from disobeying God's Word, what are we set free to do? We're set free to obey His Word. We're set free to obey His commands. We're set free to do good works.

Just as Deadguy was revived (thanks, apparently, to Dr. C and a sensible nurse) so he could go take care of his wife and kids (and dog), so you're made alive in Christ to serve those around you—to "love the Lord your God with all your heart and with all your soul and with all your strength and with all your mind, and your neighbor as yourself" (Luke 10:27).

What does it mean to love God?

Consider a couple of quotes from some really smart Christians:

"We cannot obey the Law, unless we have

been born again through the Gospel. We cannot love God, unless we have received the forgiveness of sins" (Apology of the Augsburg Confession V [III] 190). We can't love God until we're forgiven. That makes sense, because without forgiveness we're Deadguy, the enemy of God.

Here's the other:

". . . The chief worship of the Gospel is to desire to receive the forgiveness of sins, grace, and righteousness" (Apology V [III] 189). Put on those thinking caps—what desires to receive, to hold on to the forgiveness of sins?

Sounds like faith to me!

Is this great or what?

The greatest way you serve God is to keep on being forgiven!

Like I said, is this great or what?

Once forgiven, you go about your daily life, and all that you do is a good work. If you're living with your parents, doing your chores is a good work. Doing your geometry homework is a good work. Being nice to your little brother is a good work. Hey, look! All this is loving service to your neighbor!

The key to good works is forgiveness. If you're forgiven, then all that you do—unless it's against God's Word—is pleasing to God. In other words, once you have faith, good works follow.

If good works don't follow, then there's a big problem: you're killing your faith. If Jesus set you free from sin to do good works, and you're not doing them, that means all you're doing is sinning. Remember, willful sin kills faith.

That's why James 2:17 says, "So also faith by itself, if it does not have works, is dead." If someone says he is a Christian but isn't doing good works, he's fooling himself. He's really Deadguy. A Christian is set free from sin to serve. A Christian who doesn't serve is killing his faith.

156

Early Lutherans put it like this: "'Faith and good works well agree and fit together; but it is faith alone, without works, that lays hold of the blessing.' Yet it is never, ever, alone" (Formula of Concord, Solid Declaration III:41).

Faith alone saves, but faith is never alone.

Jesus said it this way: "I am the vine; you are the branches. Whoever abides in Me and I in him, he it is that bears much fruit, for apart from Me you can do nothing" (John 15:5). Our backyard is full of raspberries. As long as the branches are connected to the rest of the plant, they grow like crazy. (Sometimes, I have nightmares where they grow into the garage and try to jumpstart my car. Actually, they laugh at my car and take my wife's.) But if you lop off the branch, the berries just aren't going to happen. First things first, they have to be connected to the branch.

Jesus calls Himself the Vine. If you have been joined to Him by faith, then you bear fruit—you do good works. If you're not joined to Him, you're Deadbranch. You can't do good works, because Jesus says, "Apart from Me, you can do nothing." The things you do might help other people, but they don't please God. Therefore, they are not good works.

So, there you go: faith alone saves, but faith is never alone.

157

First comes faith, and good works follow.

Apart from Christ, you can't do any good works.

In Christ, forgiven for your sins, all that you do is pleasing to Him.

Any questions?

Q&A:
You Ask . . .

**You just wrote that whatever
a non-Christian does isn't pleasing to
God. What if a guy who wasn't
a Christian built a thousand orphanages around the world?**

Those thousand orphanages would help a lot
of kids, but they still wouldn't be good works in
God's sight, because they were done apart from
faith. Let's look at it this way: since the builder
isn't a Christian, he's not building orphanages
in service to Jesus, right? So in whose service
is he building them? To a different god? To
make a name for himself? Is he building them
because he believes there is no God, so we have
to look out for each other? Is he building them
as a tribute to his belief that man is basically

good, not sinful, and doesn't need forgiveness? In each case, his reason is one that denies the need for Jesus and forgiveness. Will his work help people? Yes. But his work doesn't please God if he doesn't acknowledge Jesus, trusting in Him for forgiveness.

So can God use non-Christians to accomplish things?

Yes. God uses all sorts of people to accomplish His will. The textbook case is back in Ezra 1, where God used King Cyrus to get His people back to Jerusalem. There's no proof that Cyrus trusted God's promised Gospel, but God used him anyway. God uses all sorts of people as His instruments to care for you. Your dentist may be a complete unbeliever, but the Lord still uses him for your good. And remember, clean teeth are happy teeth.

You said that as long as i'm forgiven, whatever i do is a good work. So if i go rob a liquor store, is that God-pleasing?

No. If you were to go for the stick-up, you'd be breaking the Seventh Commandment. You'd be stealing. A sin, by definition, is not God-

159

pleasing. It doesn't result from faith—it harms it.

in Revelation 20:12, it says that all the dead are judged according to their works. How does this agree with the Gospel that we're saved solely by Jesus and what He's done? And if we're judged by our works on the Last Day, how can we enter heaven?

Great question. Revelation 20:12 indeed says that all will be judged according to their works, both believers and unbelievers. (This also pops up at the end of the Athanasian Creed, which has thrown some people off too.) Here's the difference: those who are unforgiven still have their sin, because they've refused Jesus' gift of forgiveness. Therefore, when God looks at them, He sees their sin and their sinful works. When believers stand before God on the Last Day, they stand as those forgiven—as those whose sin has been taken away. Therefore, when God looks at believers, He doesn't see any "bad works," because they're gone for Jesus' sake. All He sees is righteousness and good—the righteousness and good that Jesus has given them.

So when you're judged as a Christian by your works on the Last Day, you're judged by what Jesus has done. He's made you and all your works good.

I've been invited to serve the Lord by going on a mission trip to Mexico. Do I have to go?

No, you don't *have* to. If you stay home, clean your room, and honor your parents, these works are just as God-pleasing as serving people in Mexico. It's not as if God gives double service points when you cross a border. What matters is that you're forgiven.

On the other hand, it's not a bad idea to go on the trip to expose yourself to a different culture, and to see the needs others have. You might better understand how much God has given you for this life, and you might learn love for your neighbor a little bit more. Either way, whatever you're doing is good before God as His forgiven child; but the trip might be more of a learning experience.

You said the "chief worship of the Gospel is the desire to receive the forgiveness of sins." Isn't telling people about Jesus more important?

161

Many people today believe and teach that the number one job of Christians is to witness. In other words, mission work is the highest priority of the Church. Here's the question: is telling other people about Jesus a good work? Absolutely! So what has to happen before you can do good works? You have to be made alive and forgiven. Forgiveness comes first—that's the chief worship of the Gospel, receiving what Jesus has done for you.

So do i have to tell other people about Jesus?

You don't *have* to—you *get* to. Look, there's no better news than the Gospel. What could be better than telling people they can live forever, for Jesus' sake, as God's forgiven people? That shouldn't be something you *have* to do—it should be something that just spouts out of you.

So why doesn't it? What makes evangelism tough for Christians today? Part of it is ignorance; you and I are good at talking about stuff we know. If you know a lot about cars or football, you can talk about it a lot. One of the big problems for Christians today is that they don't seriously, continually read and study

God's Word. Because they're unfamiliar with it, they don't know what to say. There's an easy solution: keep feeding your faith with God's Word. The more you know, the easier it is to talk about it.

Another problem is fear; you and I are afraid of rejection, scorn, and more if we speak the Gospel. It's a big temptation, and it's why Paul tells Timothy, "Therefore do not be ashamed of the testimony about our Lord" (2 Timothy 1:8) and then goes on to specify that the "testimony" is the Gospel of Jesus. If you're afraid to speak, then confess the fear. Christ has died for that sin, too, and sets you free to share His Word as the opportunity arises.

163

How do i know when i'm doing enough good works?

You can never do enough good works, because there will always be people who need help and there will always be more that you can do. So keep your eyes on the cross and Jesus' sacrifice for you. Rejoice that He's done enough to forgive you for all of your sins, and that now you're set free to serve as you are able.

How do i know what good works to do?

I'm glad you asked the question, because it raises an important point—God gives us different stations (vocations) in life, and those stations have good works attached to them. A Christian who is a police officer has the good work of arresting bad guys—if you don't have a badge, then you don't. A pastor has the good work of preaching sermons and administering the Sacraments. If you step into the pulpit when I'm about to start, we're going to have to have a talk. Likewise, if you're taking chemistry at school, the homework is your good work to do. If I did your homework for you, we'd both be guilty of cheating.

So how do you know what good works to do? Look at the vocations God has given you: child, student, worker, teammate, and so forth. You'll find enough good works to do there too. Never forget your station of "child of God for Jesus' sake," and always rejoice in your service of being forgiven.

i went to the nursing home and visited some people with my youth group, but i didn't really want to do it. Since i had a bad attitude, was that a good work?

Assuming you're a Christian, yes. Sin clings to everything we do, but Jesus has taken away all of our sins. Therefore, when God looks at you at the nursing home, all He sees is one of His righteous children—for Jesus' sake, of course—doing good.

We've looked at politics in civics class, and the whole scene looks really sleazy right now. Can a Christian be involved in politics?

Christians are commanded to support the state (Romans 13:1). In the United States, this can include holding a political office. I pray that we have godly men and women who serve in these offices, but it's not easy. Politics is all about compromise—you get some of what you want, and others get some of what they want. That means if you're a legislator, you're going to have to vote for some bad in order to get some good done. Your good works are going to look lost a lot of the time.

Again, no matter who you are, and no matter what your station, sin clings to all that you do. If you become involved in politics and government, God bless you. Work as hard as you can to do what's right, and give thanks at

165

the end of the day that your salvation is sure because of what Jesus has done, not because of what you've accomplished, or tried to accomplish. (For more on this topic, you can check out the church and state section in *You Ask about Life*.)

What are "fruits of faith"?

Fruits are works. Therefore, those who are connected to Jesus (as branches to a vine, John 15:5) produce good works (see James 3:17). These are fruits of faith because they are done by one who trusts that Jesus has forgiven him. On the other hand, false prophets are "connected" to a different god, so they produce bad fruits. Their teachings are false and to be avoided (Matthew 7:15–16).

in Matthew 7:20, Jesus says "You will recognize them by their fruits." Can i tell if someone is a Christian by the works she's doing?

You want to be a little bit careful here. Remember the orphanage builder a few questions back? Sometimes people do very helpful things, but without faith. In Matthew 7:15–20,

Jesus is talking about prophets—those who claim to speak God's Word, and the "fruits" are what they teach. He's telling us we should compare whatever doctrine we hear to His Word—that's how we'll know if the teacher is connected to Christ, the Vine.

Hey, James 2:21 says, "Was not Abraham our father justified by works when he offered up his son Isaac on the altar?" Verse 24 says, "You see that a person is justified by works and not by faith alone." So doesn't this mean people are saved by works—at least in part?

167

It sounds like it, but you've got to look at the verses in between:

> You see that faith was active along with his works, and faith was completed by his works; and the Scripture was fulfilled that says, "Abraham believed God, and it was counted to him as righteousness"—and he was called a friend of God. (James 2:22–23)

God created us to do good works, to serve Him and one another—that's what His commandments are all about (Matthew 22:37–39). If He makes us alive, but we don't do any good works with that life, then we haven't fulfilled the purpose for which He made us. That's why we say good works are necessary—but not for salvation. Good works follow salvation.

By the way, while James ties "Abraham believed God" in with the near-sacrifice of Isaac, the quote comes from Genesis 15:6, well before Isaac is even born. When did Abraham believe God? When God promised, "Look toward heaven, and number the stars, if you are able to number them. . . . So shall your offspring be" (Genesis 15:5). What was God saying? He wasn't talking about the nation of Israel; He was talking about Jesus! This wasn't the first time: in Genesis 12:3, God promised Abraham, "In you all the families of the earth shall be blessed." He was talking about all who—like Abraham—would be saved by faith in the Savior who was coming:

> Does He who supplies the Spirit to you and works miracles among you do so by works of the law, or by hearing with faith—just as Abraham "believed God, and it was counted to him as righteousness"? Know then that it is those of faith who are the sons of Abraham. And the Scripture, foreseeing that God would justify the Gentiles by faith, preached the gospel beforehand to Abraham, saying, "In

> you shall all the nations be blessed."
> So then, those who are of faith are
> blessed along with Abraham, the man
> of faith. **(Galatians 3:5–9)**

As Galatians says, this was an early promise of the Gospel. Abraham was saved by faith in Jesus, just as you are.

Do good works make faith stronger?

No. Forgiveness makes faith stronger. Your works don't.

But if you refuse to do good works, you're resisting what faith wants to do. You're sinning, right? That harms faith and makes it weaker.

169

it seems strange to me that when i go to church, we don't do much during the service. We sing hymns and stuff, but we spend a lot of time just listening. Wouldn't a worship service be an ideal place for us to do good works before God?

Remember what we learned before, that the highest worship of God is the desire to receive the forgiveness of sins. (After all, if Jesus shed

His blood to give you forgiveness, what could be more important?) For more, turn the page and we'll take a look at worship.

Section Five: Faith and Worship

A Look at Worship in the Bible

Now that we've taken a look at faith and good works, this is a good time to talk about faith and worship. I want to start out with a text from Luke that didn't make sense to me for the longest time; but when it did, it was full of good stuff. At first, it may seem to have little to do with worship; but let's give it a look:

> Now as they went on their way,
> Jesus entered a village. And a woman

named Martha welcomed Him into her house. And she had a sister called Mary, who sat at the Lord's feet and listened to His teaching. But Martha was distracted with much serving. And she went up to Him and said, "Lord, do you not care that my sister has left me to serve alone? Tell her then to help me." But the Lord answered her, "Martha, Martha, you are anxious and troubled about many things, but one thing is necessary. Mary has chosen the good portion, which will not be taken away from her." **(Luke 10:38–42)**

Two sisters were in Jesus' presence that day as He taught in their house. The Son of God—the Second Person of the Holy Trinity— was there in their home! What a guest! Martha was well aware of this special occasion, and she hustled to make Jesus' stay as comfortable as possible. (If a king were to visit, you'd at least pick your socks up off the floor, wouldn't you? How much more if God Himself were present in the flesh?) Mary, on the other hand, just sat down and listened to Him, which ticked off Martha. Really, who can blame her? Siblings scheme all the time to dump the chores on their brothers and sisters. So Martha appealed to Jesus, confident that He'd set Mary straight.

Jesus' answer was mind-boggling. He praised

173

Mary! He praised the sister who was just sitting there! Why? Because she had chosen the good portion—the "one thing necessary."

What was that one thing necessary? The Word! Jesus—the Word made flesh—was speaking His life-giving Word, and Mary was hanging on every word of it. Was Martha wrong to be worried about serving? No, Jesus doesn't say she was wrong. On the other hand, she was depriving herself of hearing the Word. And which is more necessary: hearing the Word that gives salvation or preparing food for the One who can feed five thousand with just a few loaves and fish (John 6:5–14)?

174

We could say that Mary exemplifies faith in this passage. Jesus is there, speaking His Word of forgiveness and salvation, and her faith clings to Him and His Gospel. Martha, on the other hand, is an example of works. She's doing things for Jesus, and that's not wrong. But works—even works directed to help Jesus Himself—don't save. The Gospel does. That's why Mary gets the better end of the deal.

Now obviously, this text doesn't take place at the local synagogue. It happens at a private home. I said before that it teaches us about worship, but what? Let's take a look at a few lessons.

1. Worship is to be pleasing to God.

That's a no-brainer, I hope. It wouldn't make sense to say, "Worship should do its best to arouse God's wrath." Not only is this obvious, but it's not even specifically a Christian idea. What I mean is this: in really general terms, to worship is to show reverence and honor toward a god—whoever or whatever that god might be. To worship is to do what pleases the deity—to do what the deity wants you to do. Take, for instance, a couple of examples of idol worship in the Old Testament. In 1 Kings 18, Elijah stood up against 450 prophets of Baal. As they tried to get the attention of their false (dead) god, the prophets of Baal cut themselves with lances and swords "until the blood gushed out upon them" (1 Kings 18:28); apparently, followers of Baal believed they would please their god if they shed their blood for him. Another example would be Molech, god of the Ammonites. His worshipers earned his favor by offering one of their children as a burnt sacrifice (Leviticus 18:21). Several kings of Israel sacrificed their sons in worship to Molech (see 2 Kings 16:3 and 2 Kings 21:6).

Those are two gory, ugly examples of worship of false gods. I bring them up for two reasons. For one, worship of a god means doing

175

what pleases it. If your god demands that you cut yourself or sacrifice children, that's what you've got to do to worship this false god. For another, look at the contrast between Baal and Molech vs. the one true God. Rather than require you to sacrifice a child (or anything else) to earn His help, God sacrificed His own Son to save you (John 3:16). Rather than require you to shed your blood to make Him love you, Jesus shed His blood to redeem you (1 John 1:7). That's the Gospel, right? And it runs completely counter to every other religion in the world. Every other religion teaches that you save yourself by you doing something, like keeping the rules, obeying the laws, meditating to a higher consciousness, helping people, paying money, traveling to certain places, or something else to please the god(s). In every other religion, salvation is all about what you do.

Only in Christianity does God save you by His work, by His service.

By His sacrifice.

What does this do to faith? Think this through: if salvation is all about what you do, then faith is also a work that you do. The message is, "Do this for the god—and if you have enough faith, it will accept what you do." This gives the god's leaders a built-in fall-back position when things don't go very well. Imagine a man coming to a priest of Molech and saying, "I've sacrificed my child to Molech, and he still didn't answer my prayer." The priest could just say, "Well, I guess you didn't have enough faith." How awful and satanic is that? Imagine if Christianity ran the same way: "Jesus died for you, as long as you have enough faith." How could you ever be sure you believed enough? How could you be sure you weren't just fooling yourself?

So we go back to this Good News—salvation is a free gift from God, because Jesus Christ earned it for you by His death and resurrection. Likewise, again, faith is a gift from God that holds on to Jesus. Neither faith nor salvation **177** are things you earn or come up with yourself. They are gifts God gives to you.

This truth has a profound effect on Christian worship.

2. Christian worship takes place in the presence of God.

It's true that in most religions, worship takes place at a special location—a church, a temple, a shrine, or the like. Why? Depending on the religion, it could be simply because it's a sacred space set aside for meditation. It could be because there's an altar there for sacrifices, or because images—statues—of the idol are there.

When it comes to worship of the one true God, there's something more. In Christian worship, God is present there. Not just present as in "God is present everywhere," but present in order to bless those who are worshiping. He's present in a way you can point and say, "There's God. There He is."

Think back to the book of Exodus, as the Israelites wandered through the wilderness toward the Promised Land. Every time they set up camp, the tabernacle stood at the camp's center. It was the place to worship God. The tabernacle was made with utmost care, with incredible detail, for a reason: this wasn't going to be a place where people would gather to look at a statue and worship a faraway God. Listen to what God said when He commanded the tabernacle, "And let them make Me a sanctuary, that I may dwell in their midst" (Exodus 25:8). This was going to be God's house! Rather than just remain remote in heaven, He was going to live there with them. In fact, what happened when the tabernacle was completed? It was finished in Exodus 40:33, and without delay—in the very next two verses:

> Then the cloud covered the tent of meeting, and the glory of the LORD

178

filled the tabernacle. And Moses was
not able to enter the tent of meeting
because the cloud settled on it, and
the glory of the Lᴏʀᴅ filled the tabernacle. **(Exodus 40:34–35)**

God moved into His house! He lived right
there with His people throughout their time
in the wilderness. They couldn't see Him—He
remained hidden behind a thick curtain in the
Most Holy Place, the inner room of the tabernacle. In the outer room, the Holy Place, the
priests worked. But no one went into the Most
Holy Place, except the High Priest—and then
only one day a year. That was God's throne on
earth.

179

My point is this: the tabernacle wasn't just
a place of worship because that's where the
priests worked. It was the central place of worship because God Himself was there. People
could point to the Most Holy Place and say,
"There's God. He's right in there. He lives with
us!"

Later on, long after the Israelites had
entered the Promised Land, King Solomon built
a temple for the Lord—a permanent building of
stone rather than the portable tabernacle. As
construction was underway, the Lord declared,
"I will dwell among the children of Israel and
will not forsake My people Israel" (1 Kings

6:13). What happened when it was completed? You've got it: God moved in.

> And when the priests came out of the Holy Place, a cloud filled the house of the Lord, so that the priests could not stand to minister because of the cloud, for the glory of the Lord filled the house of the Lord. **(1 Kings 8:10–11)**

The temple was the temple because that's where God lived. People came to the temple because that's where God promised to be. When Jesus called the temple "My Father's house" (John 2:16), He meant it—that's where God lived with His people.

180   This is an important part of Christian worship. The people of God worship where God is.

In fact, let's keep going into the New Testament. When Jesus became man, how does John describe it? "And the Word became flesh and dwelt among us, and we have seen His glory, glory as of the only Son from the Father, full of grace and truth" (John 1:14). The word *dwelt* comes from the same word as *tent* or *tabernacle*. Jesus "tented" or "tabernacled" among us—why? Because He was God—the Second Person of the Trinity; but instead of dwelling in a tent of cloth or a temple of stone, He was living among His people in human flesh.

Likewise, think about what Jesus is called

in Matthew 1:23—Immanuel. What does *Immanuel* mean? God with us! Not, "God is far away looking down and hoping we get a life," but "God with us." The Lord wasn't content to dwell with us by concealing His glory behind a curtain. To save us, He became flesh and dwelt among us.

From then until His crucifixion, God's people could find God present in two different places. He was still at the temple (Jesus Himself went there and called it His "Father's house," Luke 2:49), and He was also wherever Jesus was. People could point to the man named Jesus and say, "There He is. There is God, dwelling with us." They were exactly right.

181

3. God comes to His people to serve them.

During Jesus' public ministry on the way to the cross, crowds followed Him everywhere. They thronged Him. But why? What happened? Did the people do things for Him or did He do things for them? The answer is clear: Jesus cared for them. He performed miracles: He healed the sick, fed the hungry, and cast out demons. More important, He taught them His holy, saving Word. When people were gathered around Jesus, He served them! This was no fluke; after all, the people were beggars, no matter their social class. They needed healing from all sorts of diseases, and they couldn't heal themselves. Jesus could. They needed deliverance from demons, but they couldn't cast them out. Jesus could. They needed food they didn't have, so Jesus fed them. They needed forgiveness for their sins, but they couldn't take their own sins away. Jesus could. In fact, He took their sins upon Himself, carried them to the cross, and died for them (Isaiah 53:4–5).

Jesus Himself confirmed this to be the plan when He said, "The Son of Man came not to be served but to serve, and to give His life as a ransom for many" (Matthew 20:28). What a contrast from Baal and Molech, who demanded horrid sacrifices while making no promises. Jesus came specifically to save and to serve.

The Lord's plan hasn't changed. When He visits His people in worship, He is first and foremost there to serve them.

4. Because the Lord is present, worship is reverent.

Worship centers on the One who is most important—and if Jesus is present, that would be Him, not us. Because our Savior is with us, our attitudes and actions should reflect reverence and respect.

Go back to the tabernacle for a moment. I mentioned before that the high priest would only enter the Most Holy Place one day a year. He didn't choose the day: God did. It was the Day of Atonement (which still pops up on calendars as Yom Kippur, by the way.). Before entering, he went through a series of careful preparations, which included bathing, putting on certain garments, the sacrifice of a bull and a goat, the release of the scapegoat, and the lighting of incense. Once inside, there were more instructions about what to do with the incense and sacrificial blood. The high priest followed these meticulously, with good reason. God declared, "Tell [the high priest] not to come at any time into the Holy Place inside the veil, before the mercy seat that is on the ark, so that he may not die. For I will appear in the cloud over the mercy seat" (Leviticus 16:2). If the high priest entered God's presence unworthily, God would strike him down. In fact, I'm told that some Jewish tradition holds that the high priest entered the Most Holy Place with a rope tied around his ankle, so his body could be hauled out if he were to die before the Lord.

The point is this: the high priest, or anyone else, didn't just decide to do his own thing or bebop back behind the curtain whenever he wanted. God was there—the almighty, holy God who created all things and hated sin. He was there for His people, yes; not to harm them, but to forgive them. Even so, the people knew He deserved reverence.

During Jesus' public ministry on the way to the cross, how did the crowds react? Some jeered and rejected Him, sure. But those who came to Him treated Him reverently, respectfully. If they tried to take over the scene—as they did when they tried to make Him a king against His will (John 6:15), He prevented them. On the other hand, when a woman humbly sought to wash His feet, He permitted it (Luke 7:36–38). As far as the massive crowds that followed, they usually treated Him with reverence. We don't hear about huge displays of comedy or back-and-forth. They sat and listened and received.

The Lord deserves reverence. This is part of what the prophet Habakkuk was getting at when he declared, "But the LORD is in His holy temple; let all the earth keep silence before Him" (Habakkuk 2:20).

Back to Mary and Martha

So now we go back to Mary and Martha in Luke 10. Even though this was in a private home, I submit that this text is about worship because the Lord was present there with them, and He was present to serve them by teaching His life-giving Word. What was Martha doing? Trying to serve Jesus. What was Mary doing? Hearing His Word—she was being served by Jesus, which is what Jesus came to do. That's why Jesus praised Mary more, because she was submitting to His plan. He came to serve and she rejoiced to be served.

To put it another way, Jesus came and said, "I'm here today to give you the gift of salvation." Martha said, "I want to do this and that for you." In other words, Martha said no. She vetoed Jesus' plan in favor of her own. Mary, on the other hand, said, "Yes. If You've come to give me the gift of salvation, then I am here to receive it."

And that's what faith does, right? It clings to Jesus and His cross. It grabs hold of His gifts of forgiveness and salvation.

In the previous section, I gave you this quote from some early Lutherans: ". . . The chief worship of the Gospel is to desire to receive the forgiveness of sins, grace, and righteousness" (Apology V [III] 189). They also said this:

> Faith is the divine service *(latreia)*
> that receives the benefits offered by
> God. The righteousness of the Law is

the divine service *(latreia)* that offers to God our merits. God wants to be worshiped through faith so that we receive from Him those things He promises and offers.
(Apology IV [II] 49)

Read that last sentence again, "God wants to be worshiped through faith so that we receive from Him those things He promises and offers." Why? Because Jesus has shed His blood to give you those things. You can do nice things for others and not murder anyone whether Jesus has died for you or not. But forgiveness and salvation are only yours because He's gone to the cross for you. He's the "one thing necessary."

186

When it comes to worship for us today, this is *huge*.

Worship Today

Christian worship today is not primarily about what we are doing. It's about what God is doing for us. That may be old news to you. It may be mind-blowing. It may sound completely wrong. Let me say it again.

Worship is not primarily about what we are doing. It's about what God is doing for us.

At its heart, Christian worship today has a very important truth in common with worship in the Old and New Testaments: God is present with His people for their good. In the Old Testament, He was present with them in means such as the cloud of glory and the Most Holy Place. In the New Testament, He was present with them in the flesh. Remember, in both of these examples, people could point to a specific place or person and say, "Look, there He is! There's God!"

You still can. You can still point and say, "There is God." This is the miracle and joy of the means of grace.

The Word

"In the beginning was the Word, and the **187** Word was with God, and the Word was God" (John 1:1). That's how the Gospel of John begins, and it's talking about Jesus: after all, in verse 14, "the Word became flesh and dwelt among us, and we have seen His glory, glory as of the only Son from the Father, full of grace and truth." Yup, that's Jesus all right.

So Jesus is called the Word of God. The Bible is called the Word of God. Both are full of grace and truth. I used to think, "God's trying to make sure that we understand the close connection between these two. After all, the Bible is here to tell us about Jesus, and Jesus as God is the author of the Bible." But the connection is actually closer than that: Jesus is present with us in His Word. Wherever His Word is proclaimed, He's there.

Look, for instance, at Romans 10:6–9:

> But the righteousness based on faith says, "Do not say in your heart, 'Who will ascend into heaven?'" (that is, to bring Christ down) or "'Who will descend into the abyss?'" (that is, to bring Christ up from the dead). But what does it say? "The word is near you, in your mouth and in your heart" (that is, the word of faith that we proclaim); because, if you confess with your mouth that Jesus is Lord and believe in your heart that God raised Him from the dead, you will be saved.

The passage begins with a search for Jesus. Where is He? Who will get Him for us and to us? What's the answer? "The word is near you." Where is Jesus? He is as near to you as His Word. The Word you hear or read is like the temple curtain: Jesus is concealed within it, but He is there for you. That's why He also says, "For where two or three are gathered in My name, there am I among them" (Matthew 18:20). What does it mean to be gathered in the name of Jesus? Exodus 20:24 helps us out: "In every place where I cause My name to be remembered I will come to you and bless you." Where and how does God record His name—cause it to be remembered? By His Word. To be gathered in the name of Jesus is to be gathered in His Word. And what does Jesus say about Himself where two or three are gathered in His name? "There I am among them." Likewise, the Lord says in Exodus 20:24, "I will come to you and bless you." Your Savior is not far away. He is as near to you as His Word.

Or to put it another way, the Word made flesh is present in His inspired Word.

Now, we're not saying they're synonymous. Jesus is not a collection of holy writings. The Bible did not die on the cross to take away your sins. But at the same time, you can't separate them. Whenever you hear the Word of God, Jesus isn't far away, hoping you'll listen. He's present. He is right there with you to give you forgiveness, faith, and salvation.

Holy Baptism

Luther's Small Catechism says that "Baptism is not just plain water, but it is the water included in God's command and combined with God's Word" (SC, p. 23). What of God's Word should we use? Jesus tells us in

Matthew 28:19–20:

> Go therefore and make disciples of all
> nations, baptizing them in the name
> of the Father and of the Son and of
> the Holy Spirit, teaching them to
> observe all that I have commanded
> you. And behold, I am with you
> always, to the end of the age.

Because of what Jesus said, the formula for Baptism is, "I baptize you in the name of the Father and of the Son and of the Holy Spirit."

Now, we've already established that Jesus is present wherever His Word is. Therefore, He's present in Holy Baptism to give forgiveness, **190** life, and salvation. But look at something else in this text. After Jesus tells the disciples to baptize, He also tells them to teach all of His Word. Then, having spoken of Holy Baptism and His Word, what does He say? "I am with you always, to the end of the age."

It's no coincidence that He says so right there, in this text. How is He with us always, to the end of the age? In His Word! In Holy Baptism! Remember that back in the Old Testament, people could point to the Most Holy Place of the temple and say, "That's where God is for us." Today, you can point to Baptism and the Word and say, "That's where Jesus is for me!"

Holy Communion

> The Lord Jesus on the night when He
> was betrayed took bread, and when
> He had given thanks, He broke it, and
> said, "This is My body which is for
> you. Do this in remembrance of Me."
> In the same way also He took the cup,
> after supper, saying, "This cup is the
> new covenant in My blood. Do this, as
> often as you drink it, in remembrance
> of Me." **(1 Corinthians 11:23–25)**

With these "Words of Institution" Jesus
gave (*instituted*) the gift of Holy Communion,
the night before His death on the cross. He
took bread, and He added His Word, "This is
My body which is for you." He took wine and
added His Word, "This cup is the new covenant
in My blood." Remember, His Word isn't just
informative, but effective—it causes things to
happen. When Jesus said, "This [bread] is My
body," the bread wasn't just bread anymore. It
was still bread, but it was also His body. When
He said, "This cup is the new covenant in My
blood," the wine wasn't just wine anymore. As
well as wine, it was also His blood.

Can we explain that? No. It's called a
Sacrament—a mystery—for a good reason.
But that's plainly what Jesus said; so we say,
"Thanks be to God."

191

Whenever Holy Communion is celebrated according to Jesus' Word, Jesus is present there. Those who receive the Sacrament receive bread and wine, along with His body and blood. His Word is there, so He is there; and He says that in the case of Holy Communion, participants actually receive His body and blood.

By the way, that's what makes it a Holy Communion. A *communion* can be any old association or gathering of people. But Holy Communion is not just a gathering of people. Rather, it's a communion, a gathering between the people and Jesus—because He's there, present in the bread and wine, to give them forgiveness of sins. And where there is forgiveness of sins, there is also life and salvation.

Like the Word and Holy Baptism, you can point to Holy Communion and say, "This is more than a remembrance of what Jesus has done in the past. There's Jesus, working to forgive my sins."

Worship as "Divine Service"

Historically, Christian worship has centered on Jesus, as well as His presence in these means of grace. It still should today. Remember, Christian worship today is not primarily about what we are doing. It's about what God is doing for us. That's why worship is sometimes called Divine Service. God—the Divine One—comes to serve us. *He* comes to serve *us*! That blows my mind every time. Even now that He has given His life as a ransom for many, Jesus comes not to be served, but to serve.

How does He serve? By forgiving your sins! When He forgives your sins, He strengthens your faith.

Where does He serve you by forgiving your sins and strengthening your faith? In His Word, in Holy Baptism, in Holy Communion, that's where He promises to be.

I'm blessed and very grateful to serve as one of the pastors at a congregation many would **193** describe as very "traditional." We make use of a rather formal order of service called the liturgy, much of which has been used for hundreds— even a couple thousand—years. I'd like to paint with a broad brush and point out four general parts of the service:

1. We begin with the Invocation. The pastor says, "In the name of the Father and of the Son and of the Holy Spirit" (*LSB*, p. 151).

2. Then we confess our sins and hear the pastor speak the Absolution: "In the stead and by the command of my Lord Jesus Christ I forgive you all your sins in the name of the Father and of the Son and of the Holy Spirit" (*LSB*, p. 185).

3. During the next part of the service, we hear the pastor read some portions of the Bible, followed by the sermon and prayers.

4. During the final part of the service, we receive Holy Communion.

Throughout the service, we respond by singing the liturgy and hymns. Let's go back and take a closer look.

We start with the Invocation, "In the name of the Father and of the Son and of the Holy Spirit." Why? Because we were baptized in the name of the Father and of the Son and of the Holy Spirit. In worship, the first thing we do is remember what God has done for us. In Baptism, Jesus washed away our sins. He shared His death and resurrection with us (Romans 6:3–4), so we have died to sin and will rise from the dead too.

Then we confess our sins and hear the Absolution. The pastor doesn't say, "I, the pastor, forgive you." He says, "In the stead and by the command of my Lord Jesus Christ I forgive you all your sins." In other words, he says, "I'm here to tell you what Jesus says in His Word, and Jesus says, 'I forgive you all your sins.'" Now, if the pastor is speaking Jesus' Word, then who else is present? Jesus Himself! Therefore, who is forgiving you? (Not the pastor. It really doesn't help you if the pastor forgives you since he's a sinner too.) Jesus Himself is forgiving you! In this part of worship, the focus is again on what Jesus is doing in service to us.

Next, we hear some passages of Scripture, and the pastor preaches a sermon on one of those texts. The sermon had better be a proclamation of the Word, because who is present in that Word? Jesus Himself is present, giving forgiveness and strengthening faith. The purpose of Scripture readings and the sermon are to bring Jesus to you once again.

Finally, we celebrate Holy Communion. Why? You've got it—because once again, Jesus comes to us, promising that He is present with His body and blood in bread and wine. Again, **195** this part of worship is all about what Jesus is doing for you.

When people visit our church, I try to contact them afterward, thank them for coming, and ask if they have any questions. Many people express an appreciation for the formality and reverence of the service; others look at the same formality and reverence and say it felt stiff and passive, as if we weren't doing much. I can understand why they feel that way. In many Christian churches today, worship is extremely active, hip, and exciting, making use of the latest technology and music styles to communicate.

At the same time, I believe reverence is most appropriate for worship, because it reflects how people acted at the temple in the Old Testament. It follows the lead of our long-departed brothers and sisters in Christ who sat at the feet of Jesus and drank in the Word He spoke to them all day long. It falls in line with the examples of Abraham (Genesis 17:3) and the cleansed leper (Luke 17:16), who came into the presence of God and could only fall on their faces in worship. If we truly believe the Lord Himself is present, it's right to be reverent as He serves us, as we hear His Word and receive His Supper.

196

I'm also not bothered if our worship is described as passive. The One who is active is the One who is doing something, while the one who is passive is the one who is, um, being done to. The One who is active is the One who gives. The one who is passive is the one who receives. In worship, we are primarily receivers, not givers. Jesus is the giver, giving forgiveness and faith. Naturally, we respond. We offer a sacrifice of thanksgiving by our words and our singing. We contribute offerings so the bills get paid and we can keep coming to hear the Word. But first and foremost, we're there to receive.

We're there to be Mary, not Martha.

We get to be Martha for the other 167 hours

of the week, running around like beheaded chickens in service to those around us. The rest of the week is about good works, about faith active in love. Here, in worship, Jesus is present to forgive. He's present to strengthen our faith. He gathers us in to receive.

Now, last I checked, this is a book about faith, not worship; so what do worship and faith have to do with each other? Remember this quote from earlier in the chapter? "God wants to be worshiped through faith so that we receive from Him those things He promises and offers." (Apology IV [II] 49)

God wants us to receive what He promises— so much so that He's given His Son to death **197** on the cross in order to give us His gifts. What clings to Jesus and receives those gifts for Jesus' sake? Faith does! Therefore, worship and faith go together; and Christian worship is all about your faith receiving what God wants you to have: Jesus and the forgiveness of sins. Where can you find Jesus and the forgiveness of sins? In His Word. In His Sacraments. Your faith clings to these, because that's where Jesus is present. There He is, for you.

In fact, I think any decision by a congregation or individual about worship should start out with this test: "Does it point us to Jesus and the cross?" and "Does it feed our faith with

Jesus and His grace?"

Now, for whatever reason, talking about worship these days tends to get some folks a little excited. I imagine there might be a few questions, so let's see if I can give you some answers.

What's so good about liturgical worship? is it the only way to worship?

I think liturgy has several things going for it. It lends itself to reverence, and it's certainly full of God-pleasing stuff—after all, most of the liturgy is taken straight out of God's Word! More than that, though, the liturgy doesn't fail to proclaim that God is present with His people in order to serve them.

Consider, for instance, the liturgy for a service of Holy Communion. Among its songs is the *Gloria in Excelsis*, which begins, "Glory be to God on high: and on earth peace, goodwill toward men" (*LSB*, p. 187). Where do you find that in the Bible? That's what angels sang to the shepherds when Jesus was born (see Luke 2:14)—Jesus was present in Bethlehem to save His people. Later on in the liturgy comes the *Agnus Dei*, which begins, "O Christ, Thou Lamb of God, that takest away the sin of the world, have mercy upon us" (*LSB*, p. 198). Where do find this in the Bible? When John the Baptist saw Jesus coming to be baptized, he declared, "Behold, the Lamb of God, who takes away the sin of the world" (John 1:29)! Jesus was present there to serve by His Baptism. After Holy Communion, we sing the *Nunc Dimittis*, which begins, "Lord, now lettest Thou Thy servant depart in peace" (*LSB*, p. 199). Who sang it first? Simeon, in Luke 2:29–32 (KJV). Why? Because he was holding the baby Jesus in his arms—Jesus was present there to save. In between singing these songs in the liturgy, what happens? We hear God's Word and receive His Supper—Jesus is present with us to serve and to save, just as He was present with John the Baptist, Simeon, and others.

The liturgy never lets you lose sight of the purpose of worship: for you to receive forgiveness from God, who is present. So while there's no commandment that we have to use the liturgy, I don't think you could find a better form of worship.

What do you think about so-called "contemporary worship"?

I think it's fair to apply the same criteria to any sort of worship—is it God-pleasing? Does the style and the content of worship reflect the teaching that God is present and present to serve? Is the service reverent, because worshipers take into account God's presence with them? In my experiences with so-called "contemporary worship," I haven't found a clear yes to all of these questions. Instead, in my experience, contemporary worship often has originated in church bodies that deny Jesus is present to forgive in His means of grace. If that's true (and it's not), then worship changes. It's not about God coming to serve us, but it's all about us serving God. That turns worship on its head, and it doesn't help.

The other argument I've heard for contemporary worship is that it's more user-friendly for visitors, which we'll get to in the next question.

is worship for members of a church, or is it for visitors?

Worship has always been for the people of God. Look at the Old Testament. The temple worship was for Israel, although foreigners who converted could partake in some rituals. In the New Testament, while Jesus spoke His Word to all who would hear, He only celebrated the Last Supper (the first Lord's Supper) with His disciples. After His ascension, those who gathered for worship were those who were baptized, and then continued to hear His Word and receive His Supper (see Acts 2:41–42).

This makes sense. If worship is about God coming to give His gifts of grace and faith to His people, then worship is foremost for receivers—for believers! The Divine Service is the family meal. Visitors are welcome, but this is the time when the Lord gathers His children together and feeds them. In recent years, however, there's been an argument that worship should be designed primarily for visitors, not members. But this presents a lot of challenging questions, not the least of which is this: if you simplify the service for visitors, when do you feed the members with meatier stuff?

if worship is primarily for members, how are new people brought into the Church?

They're brought in because the Holy Spirit gathers them in by His Word. This may happen because they come into church, hear the Word, and want to hear more. It may happen because a friend shares the Gospel with them and invites them to church. It may be because they heard the Gospel at a relative's funeral service and believed in Jesus as the Victor over death. But bringing people in is the work of the Holy Spirit. We simply have the joy of sharing the Gospel as the opportunity arises.

203

Are hymns better than praise music?

Hmmm. Let's divide music for worship into two parts: tune and text. Evaluating the text is easy. Do the words of the song accurately proclaim the truths of Scripture? Do they properly praise God—in other words, do the words declare what God has done? Most important, do the words proclaim the Gospel? Ideally, do they also proclaim that Jesus is present with His people until He returns in glory? In general, hymns deliver God's Word better than so-called "praise music," which often strives for a simple truth or two at most. The content of good hymns (and not all hymns are good) is superior in its proclamation of Jesus.

The tune of a song is a little tougher to evaluate. Ideally, the music should serve as a good, reverent foundation for the words. (I'm always ticked off when I find a hymn with great words but a wimpy tune!) Music should fit the rest of the worship service—it should fit in with the liturgy, not sound like you've tried to build a service out of miscellaneous leftovers. Furthermore, the tune should not distract from the words or be irreverent—and I think a lot of contemporary music is designed more to be catchy for the singers than to be fitting for the presence of God.

You mentioned the tabernacle and temple. Weren't they offering sacrifices there? Weren't they doing something for God?

Not everyone made sacrifices—only the priests did. They acted as go-betweens between the Lord and the people. Why? Their work served to point to Jesus. As they offered sacrifices, they pointed to Jesus, who would offer Himself as the sacrifice for all sin—including the sins of Old Testament people (Hebrews 10:11–14). Apart from the priests, what did the people do? They offered prayers and waited while the priest worked on their behalf (Luke 1:21), even as Jesus—our eternal High Priest (Hebrews 7:26) works for us.

Aren't all Christians priests? Shouldn't they be doing things in worship?

Yes! 1 Peter 2:9 declares that all Christians are part of a royal priesthood, and priests offer sacrifices. However, since Jesus has offered the once-and-for-all sacrifice for sin, what's left for Christians to do? Offer a sacrifice of praise and thanksgiving (Hebrews 13:15), which is what we do as we sing hymns, confess creeds, and pray.

Today, people often confuse *priest* with *pastor* and think everyone should be doing what the pastor does. But the two aren't the same; a priest offers sacrifices toward God, while a pastor is called to bring forgiveness to you in Jesus' stead.

Who dwelt in the Most Holy Place?
The Father, the Son, or the Holy Spirit?

The LORD did, says the Bible (1 Kings 8:11), so why not the entire Holy Trinity? There's no reason to think otherwise.

isn't God everywhere? i feel really close to Him when i go for a hike in the forest. Why is it a big deal that He's present in His means of grace?

God is everywhere (Jeremiah 23:24), including the forest. However, He doesn't promise to forgive your sins in the forest. Let's try an illustration. What if I said to you, "I believe God is everywhere and has nourishment for my body, so I'm going to go eat a fence post"? You'd say, "But God doesn't give fence posts for nourishment. He gives food for your body, so go eat some food." Likewise, God gives forgiveness—food for faith—in His means of grace. He's everywhere, but He's present with grace in His Word and Sacraments. And isn't it extremely cool that He tells us exactly where we can find Him and His grace?

206

Why did the temple curtain tear when Jesus died?

The curtain that hid the Most Holy Place (Matthew 27:51) did in fact tear when Jesus died. This was a statement that the temple had run its course. No more sacrifices were necessary, because Jesus had made the sacrifice for our sins. Furthermore, God would no longer be present with His people in the Most Holy Place as He had been; now, He'd be present with them in His means of grace.

You said that when Jesus became flesh, He hid His glory in human flesh just as God hid His glory behind the curtain in the temple. Does that mean Jesus' body was just a covering, nothing more?

207

No, and that's a good question. Jesus didn't just wrap Himself in flesh that wasn't part of Him. John 1:14 says He *became* flesh. We're back to that mystery we talked about in section 1. Jesus is both fully God and fully human—body and all.

When my relatives came to church with us, they were appalled that the pastor

said, "i forgive you all of your sins." They said it was blasphemy. Were they right?

It sounded funny to me, too, at first, but you have to listen to the words around that statement. The pastor speaks the general absolution (or announcement of forgiveness) as part of the liturgy. A key phrase in that announcement is this: "In the stead and by the command of my Lord Jesus Christ I forgive you all your sins . . ." The pastor is speaking in Jesus' place. In other words, he's saying, "I'm here to tell you what Jesus says to you, and Jesus says to you, 'I forgive you all your sins.'"

If the pastor weren't speaking on behalf of Jesus, then it would be blasphemous. If you show up to heaven and say, "Let me in because Tim Pauls forgave me," it's not going to go very well for you. But if you say, "Let me in because Jesus forgives me (my pastor told me so!)," the gates are open.

My pastor has started to offer private confession, and the idea makes me uncomfortable. What's it for?

Sometimes you'll be guilty of some sin that really dogs you—you'll hear that you're forgiven during the worship service, for instance, but you'll still have trouble believing you're forgiven for that particular sin. In that case, private confession is a great blessing. You can go and confess that specific sin to the pastor, and he can then show you verses from Scripture that declare Jesus has died to take away this particular sin too. Your faith loves to hear that. It's a great comfort and completely confidential—the pastor cannot reveal your confession to anyone.

What should i wear to church?

You should dress in a way that conveys reverence toward God. Sloppy clothes communicate that you just don't care about the Lord and His grace, whether or not it's true. On the other hand, a formal tuxedo might be tidy, but it draws attention from God to you. Clothing for worship should be designed to communicate reverence in a way that doesn't draw attention to you.

209

At my friend's church, you have to be a certain age in order to be baptized. Why is that?

Back in section 1, we answered a question about the "age of accountability," which is the idea that you have to be certain age before you can understand enough to believe in Jesus and decide to be a Christian. We debunked this because faith is a gift of God, not a work of man. Therefore, God can give faith even to a baby.

Your friend's church almost certainly believes that faith is a decision man makes, not a gift of God. Therefore, Holy Baptism is a rite in which someone declares he's old enough to believe and follow Jesus. However, since faith is a gift of God, and because God gives faith in Baptism, it is entirely right to baptize babies. God gives infants faith in Holy Baptism.

210

This is a huge deal! If you believe faith is something you do, then you'll also believe Holy Baptism is something you do to show your faith in God. If you believe faith is something God gives, then you'll also believe Baptism is a means God uses to give it to you.

Doesn't someone have to be old enough to understand Baptism in order to receive its benefits?

No, because Holy Baptism depends on God

and His Word, not us. Let's use an illustration. Suppose it's winter, and I give a newborn baby a nice, warm sweater. Does the baby have to understand how a sweater insulates and retains heat before it will keep him warm? No, because the sweater's operation doesn't depend on the baby's understanding. Likewise, Baptism doesn't depend on the baby's understanding. God gives His gifts of grace and faith, and the baby benefits.

i was baptized as a baby, and then later i just stopped believing in Jesus for a while. Do i need to be baptized again?

No. In Baptism, the Lord brought you into His family—He adopted you. When you abandoned the faith, you ran away from home for a while. Now that you're back, you don't have to be re-adopted or re-baptized. Even if you abandoned God for a while, He never abandoned the promises He made to you when He baptized you, and that's what matters.

i was reading the Bible, and came across John 14:23: "Jesus answered him, 'if anyone loves Me, he will keep My word, and My Father will love him,

and We will come to him and make Our home with him.'" it sounds like Jesus is saying that He is present with us because of our work of obeying His Word. Can you explain?

The key word is *keep*, which can mean *obey* in English—as in, "I keep the rules." In Greek, though, it has more of a sense of "hold on to," "keep watch over" maybe even "treasure." When Jesus tells us to keep His Word, He is telling us to hold on to it, guard it, keep it close. Why? Because that's His means of grace— that's how He's present with us. If you hold on to His Word (which you do by faith, not by your work), Jesus is with you. If you reject it, you've rejected Him.

Why do Christians disagree so sharply about Holy Communion?

Sad, isn't it? The devil must delight that Christians divide over Baptism and Communion, two of the means by which Jesus is present with His people.

At the heart of the disagreement is the little word *is*. When Jesus took the bread and broke it at the Last Supper, He told His disciples,

"This is My body." Likewise with the cup, He said, "This cup is the new testament in My blood" (See 1 Corinthians 11:24–25, KJV). In the Lutheran Church, we take Jesus at His Word. We believe that in Holy Communion, the bread is both bread and His body, and the wine is both wine and His blood.

Many Christians object to this, arguing that Jesus *meant* to say, "This [bread] symbolizes My body" and "This cup symbolizes the new testament in My blood." Based on this interpretation, they argue that the bread and wine are only symbols—reminders—of Jesus, but that He's not present in the bread and wine. Therefore (and this is huge!), Holy Communion isn't about Jesus coming to serve us with forgiveness. Instead, it's about us gathering together to show our commitment to Him. The Lord's Supper gets turned from His work to our work. Sadly, that's the position of most Protestant denominations.

We could write books about this disagreement, but I'll offer a few short points:

1. If Jesus meant to say *symbolize*, why didn't He say it? Why did He say *is* when He knew He could be clearer and could foresee the trouble that would come?

2. The argument that Jesus meant *symbolizes* or *rep-*

213

resents is largely based on an axiom, "The finite is not capable of containing the infinite." In other words, you can't put the infinite Son of God into a finite piece of bread. That's great physics, but it's crummy theology. You will not find this saying in the Bible—but it does sound an awful lot like Plato. It's not a good idea to use a secular Greek philosopher to decide what Jesus meant to say.

3. An oft-overlooked text about Holy Communion is 1 Corinthians 10:16: "The cup of blessing that we bless, is it not a participation [a communion] in the blood of Christ? The bread that we break, is it not a participation [a communion] in the body of Christ?" In Greek, these questions are structured to indicate that the answer is yes. You can't participate in the body and blood of Christ if He isn't there with His body and blood.

4. One more. God has been present with His people, outside of them, throughout history—think the pillar of cloud, the Most Holy Place, and Jesus in the flesh. Why would He not continue to be present with them now? Why could He not in bread and wine?

When Jesus said *is*, He meant *is*. In Holy Communion, we receive His body and blood for the forgiveness of sins.

Do Lutherans believe in transubstantiation?

Now, there's your big word for the day. Transubstantiation is the teaching that in Holy Communion, the bread and wine turn into Jesus' body and blood so there's no bread and wine left. It looks like bread and wine, but it's not. This is the teaching of the Roman Catholic Church. How did they get it? They got it from Aristotle, yet another secular Greek philosopher.

Lutherans don't believe in transubstantiation. Rather, we believe that in Holy Communion we receive Jesus' body and blood as well as bread and wine.

Between this question and the last one, we've staked out three positions on the Lord's Supper: you receive (1) only bread and wine (most Protestants), (2) only Jesus' body and blood (Roman Catholics), or (3) all of the above (Lutherans). The third position is the one that best agrees with Scripture, "The bread that we break, is it not a participation in the body of Christ?" (1 Corinthians 10:16). Here, St. Paul makes clear that the bread is still bread, yet also the body of Jesus.

if a church rewrites the Words of institution to say, "This represents My body," is Jesus still present in

Holy Communion?

No, because they're no longer using His Word. They've changed it into their own interpretation. Even if they say "This is My body," but make it clear they believe *is* means *represents* or *symbolizes*, they're no longer using His Word. They've changed the Supper from God's work for us to our work of devotion for Him.

This is actually sort of a blessing. If Jesus were present in that rite, then all who partake would be guilty of not discerning His body (1 Corinthians 11:29) and receive it to their judgment. This way, they're spared.

We also note that, in many of these churches, the Word of God is still read and proclaimed. Therefore, the Holy Spirit is at work elsewhere in the service to give faith and forgiveness to those He has gathered there.

My friend's pastor said we're cannibals because we believe Jesus is present in the bread and wine. i was speechless—is this true?

No. What receives bread and wine into you? Your mouth does. What receives Jesus into you? Your faith does, right? Faith clings to

216

Jesus and the forgiveness He gives. Your faith doesn't receive bread and wine, and your mouth doesn't receive Jesus. You're not a cannibal. If it makes you feel any better, early Christians were accused of cannibalism for believing the same thing you do. Their accusers were wrong then too.

What does faith have to do with Holy Communion? is Jesus present because i believe He's there?

No. It sounds like you've heard a teaching called *receptionism*, which in general teaches that people only receive Jesus in the Supper when they believe He's there. If that's the case, your faith decides whether Jesus is present. Does that sound right? Hardly! Jesus' presence is all His doing. Therefore, everyone who receives Holy Communion receives Jesus.

217

Can you explain the practice of "closed Communion"? My aunt was really mad when the pastor wouldn't let her commune at our church.

1 Corinthians 11:27–29 says:

> Whoever, therefore, eats the bread

or drinks the cup of the Lord in an unworthy manner will be guilty concerning the body and blood of the Lord. Let a person examine himself, then, and so eat of the bread and drink of the cup. For anyone who eats and drinks without discerning the body eats and drinks judgment on himself.

Since we don't want to bring harm to people, we don't want to commune people without first making sure they're prepared for the Lord's Supper. Some of the questions that arise are these:

218

1. Does the individual believe he is a sinner in need of forgiveness? If not—if he's unrepentant of some sin, he's not coming to the altar for the right reason and isn't ready.

2. Does the individual believe Jesus is present in the Supper, with His body and blood in the bread and wine? Doubting Jesus' presence—not "discerning the body," as 1 Corinthians 11:29 says—makes one unworthy of receiving Holy Communion. That should be obvious: in the Lord's Supper, Jesus says, "Here I am," and the individual is saying, "No, You're not." Rather than coming to his Savior for forgiveness, he's coming for a different reason.

3. Does the individual's confession of faith agree with this congregation's confession of faith? By communing at a church, you're declaring that you

agree with everything taught at that church (Acts 2:42). If you disagree with what that church teaches, you're giving a false impression that you support everything they say; and if the pastor admits you to the Supper, he's giving a false impression that he supports all you believe. A pastor needs to know that you're in full agreement before he can commune you in good conscience.

4. No matter what the individual believes, does he belong to a church body that agrees with this congregation's confession of faith? The reasoning is the same as number three above.

I don't know what happened with your aunt, but I hope she respected the pastor's request that she wait. I bet he asked to speak with her **219** more. Anyway, isn't it just good manners for a visitor to abide by a church's practice and a pastor's request to be careful, especially when that practice is scriptural and designed to look out for the visitor's well being?

But isn't the pastor judging the person's heart when he asks them not to commune?

No. Pastors don't have x-ray, heart-judging vision. That's why they need to talk to people first before they admit them to the altar, and make a decision based on what the people say.

If pastors did have heart-judging abilities, no such conversations would be necessary.

Sometimes, I've heard 1 Corinthians 11:25 translated as "this cup is the new covenant in My blood" (ESV), and sometimes "this cup is the new testament in My blood" (KJV). Is there a difference between a covenant and a testament?

A covenant is an agreement between two parties, and there are different types. Some covenants call for both parties to do something to keep the deal, while other covenants are one-sided in action—one party pledges to do something for the other.

In its most common meaning, a testament is a one-sided deal, as in "last will and testament." It's a document that stipulates what someone is giving to someone else after he dies (Hebrews 9:16). If your long-lost weird uncle dies and leaves you something in his will, it's not like you can get the will revised. What's done is done.

Testament is a better translation for 1 Corinthians 11:25. Jesus gave the gift of Holy Communion the night before His death— it was His last will and testament before He died. Furthermore, when we use *testament*, we clarify that the forgiveness Jesus gives in Holy Communion is a one-sided deal. Jesus did all the work to earn it for us. We don't work to be forgiven, but simply receive it as His heirs.

- - - - - - - - - - - - - - - - - - -

It is most astonishing that worship is about God coming to us, to give us forgiveness. In the Divine Service, the Divine One comes to serve us! That may set people back at first, but remember this is the worship of Jesus, who declared, "The Son of Man came not to be served but to serve, and to give His life as a ransom for many" (Matthew 20:28). Jesus doesn't change. He's given His life to ransom you. Even now in worship, He comes to serve you. Wow!

Section Six: Faith and Prayer

Of the many blessings God pours out upon us, I think prayer might be the most misunderstood. We want to talk about prayer in this book because faith and prayer go together—there's little dispute on this statement. But just how do they go together? Let's start out with a trip to the Pauls' household. I won't even charge you admission this time, so please don't send me a bill if this is traumatic for you.

My wife and I have two boys. They're our boys because we sorted through a lot of applications that little boys submitted and decided which ones would be the best at doing our work around the house while we sat back and ate peeled grapes. No, wait. It didn't work that way. They're our boys because they were born to us. God gave them to us. Our sons can never say, "We've earned the right to be the sons of Tim and Teresa," because they didn't do anything to earn it. (They also can't say, "What did we ever do to deserve this nightmare?")

We have rules in our house just like any family. Our boys know us pretty well by now, and they know what to expect. They can expect that we'll do our best to keep them fed and safe and healthy. So if they were to ask, "Can we have dinner today?" the answer will almost certainly be yes. We'll always give them food.

On the other hand, if they walk up and say, "Can we have a ravenous, boy-eating wildebeest for a pet?" they can be sure the answer is no. We're not here to do whatever they want, because at least for now it's true that father and mother know best. If they ask for something potentially harmful, we're going to say no for their own good.

In between are things they may or may not get. If they ask for, say, a telescope, the answer is maybe. It might show up under the Christmas tree. It might not. We haven't prom-

223

ised to buy them a telescope. Then again, we haven't promised not to buy them one either.

I don't do this for everyone. If the neighbor's boy from down the street were to come to the door and ask me for gifts, I'd kindly tell him to go home to his own parents. My boys get my attention because, well, they're my boys.

Sometimes, I admit, I yank their chain. Maybe I've told them that we're going to the local airstrip to see a classic World War II plane on display. The day arrives, they ask what time we're leaving, and I pretend ignorance: "Who said we're doing that?" The chorus is immediate: "You said so! You promised!" After they've reminded me of my promise a few times, we pack up the car and go.

224

That's just how it works; our kids know that there are some things they will get from us, some things they won't, and some things they might. They've done nothing to earn this relationship; it happened because they happened to be born to us. That was all God's doing.

What Prayer is

As a Christian, you have the privilege of speaking to God and the certainty that He listens to you. That's what prayer is. If you spend some time meditating on this statement, it's pretty astonishing. I can't get people to return my calls half the time, but the Lord of heaven and earth grants me an audience whenever I see fit to speak to Him. He desires to hear from you and me so much that He's sacrificed His Son on the cross to make it so.

Now if you have the opportunity to speak to the almighty Creator of all things, you probably want to pick your words carefully. But what should you say?

First, we'd better get the relationship down, because this is also astounding. God doesn't want to be known to you only as the almighty Creator of all things or the Lord of heaven and earth who could squash you like a bug. He doesn't say that His relationship with you is king/peasant, boss/employee or general/private. It's not master/slave. It could be if He wanted, but that's not what He wills. The Lord specifically declares, "For you did not receive the spirit of slavery to fall back into fear, but you have received the Spirit of adoption as sons, by whom we cry, 'Abba! Father!'" (Romans 8:15). He says that your relationship with Him is Father/son. (If you're a girl, it's still Father/son. In the Bible, sons got the inheritance while daughters were married off and sent away to other families. God isn't going to send you off and away to another household. You're an heir

225

of His kingdom and thus you are a *son* of God. If that still sounds odd to you, consider this: I'm a man, and the Bible says I'm part of the bride of Christ. I'd look terrible in a gown and heels; but being part of the bride means that Jesus had cleansed me from sin and made me His own, so I have no objection.)

God calls Himself your Father and—because Jesus died for you—considers you His beloved child. That's the relationship, and this also helps us understand prayer: we speak to God as a child speaks to a loving father. So with that, we'll look at Jesus' words in Luke 11:9–13:

> And I tell you, ask, and it will be given to you; seek, and you will find; knock, and it will be opened to you. For everyone who asks receives, and the one who seeks finds, and to the one who knocks it will be opened. What father among you, if his son asks for a fish, will instead of a fish give him a serpent; or if he asks for an egg, will give him a scorpion? If you then, who are evil, know how to give good gifts to your children, how much more will the heavenly Father give the Holy Spirit to those who ask Him!

"Ask, and it will be given to you." Be careful; some use this as proof that God is the ultimate vending machine, just waiting to give you whatever you want, no matter what. But remember the relationship—this is a son asking for something from his father. If one of my sons asks me for a live grenade, I'm going to listen to his request, but I'm not going to give it to him. Why? Because my wife would kill me! No, wait. That's true enough, but not part of the illustration. I'm not going to give him a live grenade because that's not what's best for him. If he asks me for some food or some time because he needs to talk, then he's got it. These things are good for him, and I've told him he can expect these things from me.

Here's an important thing about prayer:

We can pray with confidence that God will **227** answer our prayers when we ask for what He's promised to give us.

That's what Jesus says in John 16:23: "Truly, truly, I say to you, whatever you ask of the Father in My name, He will give it to you." *In My name* means "according to My Word." Whatever you ask from God that He has promised in His Word, you can be sure He will give it to you.

Therefore, knowing God's Word is an essential preparation for prayer. After all, if we don't know what God promises, how can we ask for it? But as we hear and meditate on God's Word,

He's teaching us His promises and strengthening our faith to trust in Him. This prepares us to pray, confident that God will do what He says.

So, can I pray that God would forgive me for all of my sins because Jesus died for me? Absolutely! I can pray that with confidence, because God promises that He always has forgiveness for me. Can I pray for a new Ferrari? I can, but God has never promised to give me one. If I'm sick, can I pray to God for help and trust that He will heal me? Yes! Although while God promises to heal me, He doesn't promise a timeline. If I'm sick, He might heal me today, or He might heal me on the Last Day. Either way, though, He keeps His promise—and our Father knows best.

This is the key to prayer: it's all about the promises of God. It's saying, "Dad, You promised!" When you ask God for what He has promised in His Word, you can be sure you will receive, because God is always faithful. His answer may not be on your schedule, or quite what you envision. Don't be disappointed, because it will be better. Remember the last part of Luke 11:9–13: if I—a sinful man and not exactly the brightest bulb—know how to give good things to my kids (they are still alive and well, after all), then how much more will God give to you?

Even better, look specifically at the text, "If you then, who are evil, know how to give good gifts to your children, how much more will the heavenly Father give the Holy Spirit to those who ask Him" (Luke 11:13)! God gives the Holy Spirit! The Holy Spirit gives forgiveness and—drum roll, please—you know it's coming by now, don't you . . . faith! And if you have received grace and faith, then all of God's blessings are yours!

Faith and Prayer

Where does faith come into this? Remember what faith does: it clings to Jesus and the forgiveness He's won on the cross. This has some important implications for prayer.

229

1. Because of that forgiveness, you're God's beloved child and He's your Father; and because you're God's beloved child, you can be certain your Father delights to hear your prayers. Furthermore, you can be certain He will answer your prayers in the way that's best for you.

2. Because faith clings to Jesus and His merit, it doesn't cling to you and yours. (You're Deadguy apart from Christ, remember?) This means that when you pray, you don't ask God to help you because you're hot stuff or because you feel you've earned His help. Instead, by faith, you pray that

God would help you for the sake of Jesus.

3. Because your faith clings to Jesus (the Word made flesh) you believe the written Word (the Bible) to be true. Therefore, by faith you believe the faith, right? You trust the Word—you trust that God's promises are true. And therefore you know what to ask for in prayer, because you know and trust the promises of God.

By faith you know that God has made you His child for Jesus' sake. That's why your Father in heaven delights to hear you pray, "But Dad, You promised!"

I'm told that Martin Luther said that prayer was all about rubbing the promises of God in His ears, of "trapping" God with His own words. He drew the picture of God like an earthly Father, waiting for us to say, "You promised, so You have to do this!" At the same time, He waits to make sure we're asking by faith—for the sake of Jesus who died for us.

One of my favorite miracles is found in Matthew (we'll look more at faith and miracles in the next chapter):

> And Jesus went away from there
> and withdrew to the district of Tyre
> and Sidon. And behold, a Canaanite
> woman from that region came out
> and was crying, "Have mercy on me,
> O Lord, Son of David; my daughter

is severely oppressed by a demon."
But He did not answer her a word.
And His disciples came and begged
Him, saying, "Send her away, for she
is crying out after us." He answered,
"I was sent only to the lost sheep of
the house of Israel." But she came and
knelt before Him, saying, "Lord, help
me." And He answered, "It is not right
to take the children's bread and throw
it to the dogs." She said, "Yes, Lord,
yet even the dogs eat the crumbs that
fall from their masters' table." Then
Jesus answered her, "O woman, great
is your faith! Be it done for you as you
desire." And her daughter was healed
instantly. **(15:21–28)**

231

It's a strange-sounding story. Jesus ignores the woman, then calls her a dog. What's up with that?

For starters, the woman is a Canaanite. She's not Jewish. She comes to Jesus and calls Him "Son of David" (15:22). That's a very Jewish thing to say. Because of that, and because of the conversation that follows, some have suggested that the woman believes Jesus will only answer her prayer if He thinks she's Jewish like Him. This isn't a huge stretch. For one thing, it was common in Bible times to believe that each nation had its own gods, so the Jewish God would only bless Jews. For another, race relations at the time weren't exactly the best, so perhaps she feared a Jewish healer wouldn't help a Canaanite.

Whatever the reason, though, it appears the woman is praying under false pretenses. She's thinking Jesus' help depends on who she is—not on who He is. So she pretends to be someone else and effectively says, "Lord, You have to help me because I'm Jewish like You!"

Jesus ignores her. Why? Because at this point, she's not praying by faith. She's not clinging to Him—she's trusting in her own plan to earn His help. So He doesn't answer her prayer. She persists, though, until He finally says, "I was sent only to the lost sheep of the house of Israel" (15:24). In other words, "The jig is up. I know who you are—and I know who you're not. So if you're trying to get Me to help you because of who you're pretending to be, it's not going to work."

The woman doesn't go away. Stripped of her pretense, she kneels and repeats her plea, "Lord, help me" (15:25). Jesus prods her a little more, "It is not right to take the children's bread and throw it to the dogs" (15:26). That sounds harsh, although *dogs* was slang for Gentiles back then. Jesus is saying, "If I'm only here to help the Jews—as you apparently believe—it's not right for Me to spend time helping Gentiles."

The woman responds, "Yes, Lord, yet even the dogs eat the crumbs that fall from their masters' table" (15:27). Something has changed—suddenly, Jesus praises her for her great faith! Why? Because by faith, she understands her position. She understands Jesus. She understands the nature of prayer and God's promises. Here's what she says: "I'm done pretending to be someone else to earn Your help. If You say I'm a dog, then I'm a dog because You say so. I can't earn Your help by being me or anyone else. But Jesus, You've promised! You've promised to help Gentile dogs like me! I believe You're the Savior, and God promised You would be the Savior of the nations (see Genesis 22:18 and Galatians 3:8). There! You promised! You have to help me, because You always keep Your promises!"

233

No wonder Jesus praises her for great faith. She clings to Him and His grace. She knows He will help because of who He is; and Jesus heals her daughter instantly. (As far as that goes, make sure you read the next, Faith and Miracles.)

That's what faith does, right? It clings to Jesus and His grace. That's how faith prays, "Father, because Jesus died for me, I'm Your forgiven, beloved child. Because I'm Your child,

You've got to help me, because You've promised."

And God always keeps His promises!

Now that we know what the relationship between faith and prayer is, we need to take a look at what it isn't.

Getting Faith and Prayer Wrong

A popular belief in society is that the strength of our faith makes prayer work, or that prayer is more effective when we're more fervent. There's the sequined caricature of television evangelism, where the preacher declares something like, "God will give you whatever you want, as long as you have enough faith. It's yours if you only believe! Name it and claim it from God for you!" In that scheme, prayer is seen as a way to get what you want from God—and as long as you have enough faith, God will give it to you. If you don't get what you pray for, you obviously didn't have enough faith. But if your faith is strong, God has to give you what you want because strong belief is just so overpoweringly impressive He has to reward it. (A side effect of this is that God is seen as the complete doofus-father who's out to spoil his kids and ruin them.) People will quote Bible verses to back it up. Here are a couple:

"In that day you will ask nothing of Me. Truly, truly, I say to you, whatever you ask of the Father in My name, He will give it to you." (John 16:23)

And Jesus answered them, "Truly, I say to you, if you have faith and do not doubt, you will not only do what has been done to the fig tree, but even if you say to this mountain, 'Be taken up and thrown into the sea,' it will happen. And whatever you ask in prayer, you will receive, if you have faith."
(Matthew 21:21–22)

So some would say that I'll get what I want from God, as long as I have enough faith.

Now, for experimental purposes, I'm willing **235** to give this a shot. Just for your edification, I'm willing to risk losing my current car in order to test this theory of faith and prayer. So please excuse me for a moment while I stop and pray that the Lord would give me a Ferrari to drive instead. (I think every pastor should drive a luxury sports car. At least, I believe that I should, though I'd have it painted in muted colors to show I'm a humble servant.) So I shall now take a moment to utter that prayer. Then I'll step out into the garage to see what's happened. After all, I have faith. Remember, I'm doing this for you. Take a break and grab a quick snack. I'll be right back . . .

I've now returned from my garage, and the experiment has not gone well. All I found was my old, used Toyota Corolla. This means one of three things.

1. My aging Corolla is now really a new Ferrari if I believe it is, although my eyes will still see a Corolla and hear a 4-cylinder engine that sounds like wheezing gerbils when I pull into traffic.

2. I don't have enough faith for a Ferrari. I only have enough faith in God to get a used Toyota Corolla. With a cracked windshield. And rear windows that no longer go up and down. That's disconcerting. If that's the case, do I have enough faith to get into heaven? (That question by itself should get you thinking!)

3. I've got the wrong understanding of faith.

The answer, of course is number three. Nowhere does God say He'll give us whatever we want as long as we believe hard enough.

First off, remember what faith does: it clings to Jesus and the forgiveness of sins. It grabs it for us so we're alive in Christ. Does faith cling to a Ferrari? No. Does it work to gratify my selfish desires? No. In fact, faith clings to the forgiveness I need because of my selfish desires!

But what about those verses I just quoted

that say God will give me whatever I ask? In these texts, Jesus doesn't say He'll give us whatever our little ol' sinful hearts desire. He says something quite different. We already looked at John 16:23 and learned that "in My name" means "according to My Word." You can't separate Jesus' name from His Word. The two go together. When Jesus tells us to pray in His name, He's telling us to pray according to His Word. In other words, He's telling us to pray what His Word says.

In our other verse, Jesus said,

> Truly, I say to you, if you have faith and do not doubt, you will not only do what has been done to the fig tree, but even if you say to this mountain, "Be taken up and thrown into the sea," it will happen. And whatever you ask in prayer, you will receive, if you have faith. **(Matthew 21:21–22)**

237

This is absolutely true, as long as you remember that faith is what clings to Jesus and His forgiveness. If you're clinging to forgiveness, you're shunning sin, right? You can't be repentant and unrepentant at the same time, after all. Therefore, if you're clinging to forgiveness, you're not going to be praying, "Dear God, here's what I want You to give me." Prayer isn't selfish, because selfishness is a sin and faith clings to forgiveness. Therefore, a prayer of faith always says, just like Jesus prayed, "Not as I will, but as You will" (Matthew 26:39). By faith, you believe that whatever the Lord does is best for you (Romans 8:28).

In other words, would it make sense for Jesus to say, "Coveting a sports car and being dissatisfied with what I've given you are both sins that you need to repent of; but since you asked for the Ferrari in prayer, I'll give in to your coveting and get you the wheels"? No. That would be like me saying, "Well, boys, I really don't think that ravenous wildebeests are appropriate gifts for Christmas. But since you really want them, I'll get 'em for you."

238

Jesus Teaches Prayer

Jesus talked about prayer, as He does here in Matthew 6. We'll look at it in two parts.

> And when you pray, you must not be like the hypocrites. For they love to stand and pray in the synagogues and at the street corners, that they may be seen by others. Truly, I say to you, they have received their reward. But when you pray, go into your room and shut the door and pray to your Father who is in secret. And your Father who sees in secret will reward you. And when you pray, do not heap

up empty phrases as the Gentiles do,
for they think that they will be heard
for their many words. Do not be like
them, for your Father knows what you
need before you ask Him.
(Matthew 6:5–8)

Jesus warns about misusing prayer. Prayer is about you and God—about you speaking to your Father in heaven. It's not something you use to show people how incredibly spiritual you think you are, as a way of saying, "Look what a great child of God I am [compared to you]." Jesus calls that hypocritical. Why? Because a child of God doesn't glory in his own greatness—he has none. If Jesus hadn't saved him, he'd be Deadguy. When you use prayer to show off to others how holy you think you are, you're not a penitent sinner asking God to fulfill His promises. You're expecting God to reward you because you're just such a great person. Now, think back to the Canaanite woman in Matthew 15. As long as she pretends to be someone she's not, Jesus doesn't give her the time of day. If you think God hears prayer because you've earned His ear and answer, then don't expect a response; as Jesus says, you already have your reward.

That's why Jesus advises you to pray in secret if you're tempted to misuse prayer to

239

draw attention to yourself. If you're all alone, there's no one around to impress. If you're alone in prayer, it's just between you and the Lord.

Jesus also warns about piling on a bunch of empty, flowery phrases, as if these would impress God and He'd listen because you're such a great speaker. Once again, why does God hear your prayers—because you get His attention by your impressive vocabulary and the one-liner you threw in, or because you're His child? It's because you're His child, of course. Next question: are you His child because you've earned it, or because Jesus has died for you and forgiven your sins? Again, it's all because of Jesus.

Therefore, let's make this absolutely clear: God hears your prayers for Jesus' sake. He does not hear your prayers because of your work or anybody else's. This means that God does not hear your prayers because

- you were very, very precise in your choice of words;

- you were feeling very earnest and sincere when you prayed;

- you prayed the same prayer over and over and over;

- you prayed in Latin;

- you prayed out loud;

- you went to church and behaved really well for two hours before you prayed;

- you got a bunch of other people to pray with you in a big group;

- you got a bunch of other people to pray with you all over the world;

- of anything else you've done.

God does not hear your prayer because of anything you've done to earn His ear. He hears your prayer because Jesus has made you His child by His death and resurrection. This is good news, because it all depends on Jesus! **241** There will be times when you stumble all over your words or don't even know how to pray. There will be times when no one is praying but you. It doesn't matter. What matters is that you're forgiven for Jesus' sake; therefore, God is going to hear your prayers. He waits and delights to hear your prayers because Jesus died for you! In fact, as Jesus says, He already knows what you need, and He delights to give it to you.

Faith and Prayer: The Lord's Prayer

Again Jesus goes on to speak about prayer

by saying:

> Pray then like this: "Our Father in heaven, hallowed be Your name. Your kingdom come, Your will be done, on earth as it is in heaven. Give us this day our daily bread, and forgive us our debts, as we also have forgiven our debtors. And lead us not into temptation, but deliver us from evil."
> **(Matthew 6:9–13)**

In giving us the Lord's Prayer, Jesus Himself teaches us how to pray. You know the text well already, so I'd like to point out a few things about it.

242 First, He tells us to call God our "Father." Right at the start, He reminds us that God doesn't help us because we've earned it. He helps us because we're His kids.

Second, the prayer is divided into seven *petitions* or requests. Every one of these petitions is based on the promises of God. God promises to make His name holy among us—and so to make us holy—by the proclamation of His Word (John 17:17). He promises that His kingdom comes now because Jesus—our King—comes to us in His means of grace (Matthew 18:20). He promises that His will is done for us (Romans 8:28), and that He provides daily bread, or all that we need for this life (Psalm 145:15–16).

He further promises to forgive us our trespasses (1 John 1:9), guard us from temptation (1 Corinthians 10:13), and deliver us from evil (Job 5:19). There are a lot more promises to back up the Lord's Prayer, but this shows you at least one for each petition.

Third, look at the content of those petitions. Only one out of seven petitions is about stuff we need for life in this world: "Give us this day our daily bread." With those seven words, we ask God for "everything that has to do with the support and needs of the body," as Luther says in the Small Catechism (p. 21). (By the way, Luther does a great job of describing the promises of the Lord's Prayer in the Small Catechism.) What do the rest of the petitions—six out of seven—have to do with? Faith and the faith! How does God make His name holy among us, send His kingdom among us, and work His will for our salvation? By His Word, which proclaims the faith and gives us faith! Likewise, He forgives us our trespasses, strengthens us against temptation (by strengthening our faith), and delivers us from all evil ultimately by the grace that Jesus has won for us.

It's an oft-overlooked lesson from the Lord's Prayer. You and I tend to focus on our daily needs for this body. In the prayer Jesus gives,

He spends six-sevenths of the time praying about faith. If you don't throw away God's daily-bread gifts for this body, you've got what you need for a while. If you don't throw away God's gifts of faith and forgiveness, you've got what you need for now and eternity.

All of the petitions of the Lord's Prayer are summed up in the third, "Thy will be done." That's a prayer of faith. That's what Jesus prayed in the Garden of Gethsemane, just before His arrest and death on the cross. "My Father, if it be possible, let this cup pass from Me; nevertheless, not as I will, but as You will" (Matthew 26:39). Facing the brutality of the scourge and the cross, as well as—infinitely worse!—suffering God's judgment for the sins of the world, Jesus made clear that He didn't desire the suffering. But He trusted His Father's will for your salvation, and He prayed "Thy will be done." Despite His looming death, He could faithfully pray, "I shall not die, but I shall live, and recount the deeds of the LORD. The LORD has disciplined me severely, but He has not given me over to death" (Psalm 118:17-18). In other words, "Father, You promised!" His Father kept His promise, and Jesus rose again on the third day.

"Thy will be done." That's a tough prayer to pray—we'll see that more in the next chapter.

Praying "Thy will be done" necessarily means praying "not as I will." But by faith, you have this certainty: for Jesus' sake, God delights to hear your prayers, and He always answers them in the way that is best for you.

There's more we could talk about regarding prayer, but we've got enough to get started; and I'm thinking a lot of your questions will fill in the blanks from here. Let's go.

Q&A:
You Ask . . .

246

is prayer more effective if a lot people are praying the same prayer?

No. If it were, it would depend on how many people you got to pray—not on the promises of God. In that case, prayer would be based on your popularity and recruiting skills, not Jesus' faithfulness to you. Does that mean it's wrong or useless to ask others to pray for you? Not at all! Like you, they have the privilege of speaking God's promises back to Him—and praying for you is one way they can act in service to others by faith.

Which is better: a prayer that's been written down and used again and again, or a prayer somebody makes up on the spot?

The quality of a prayer doesn't depend on its age, but on whether it accurately prays the promises of God. An old prayer that's been repeated a thousand times may get God's Word wrong, while a brief spontaneous prayer might get it right.

That said, I want to put in a plug for prayers that aren't made up on the spot. You can find them in hymnals, prayer books, and elsewhere. They've stood the test of time—a lot of Christians have examined them, used them, and have acknowledged that they reflect God's promises. This has advantages: sometimes when I make up a prayer on the spot, I misspeak and have to correct myself. Furthermore, when I'm really tired or grieved, I really appreciate the help of pre-written prayers to help me know what to pray.

247

Like creeds, prayers that repeat God's promises don't get stale or die with age. The Lord's Prayer certainly hasn't. If we find that such prayers don't say what we want, we need to reconsider what we're asking for.

is prayer more effective when i'm really earnest while i pray?

No, because then prayer would depend on your level of emotional commitment, not on the promises of God. Please don't misunderstand me. I'm not trying to justify an idea that we should pray as apathetically and indifferently as possible. Rather, there will be times when you're so beaten up that you can barely put together a three-word prayer. You won't have any energy left to be fervent or earnest. But as long as that prayer is built on God's promises, God will hear and answer.

So do you have any three-word prayers handy?

Yes: "Lord, have mercy," also known as the *Kyrie* in the liturgy. Even when you don't know what else to pray, you do know God has promised to be merciful to you for Jesus' sake. "Lord, have mercy" is a great prayer.

in Luke 18:1—8, Jesus tells the story of the persistent widow, who keeps on bothering the judge until he grants her request. is prayer more effective if

you ask about . . . FAiTH

i pray the same prayer again and again?

No, because then prayer would depend on your persistence, not on God's promises. In Luke 18, the judge is unjust and only answers the widow because she keeps bugging him. Jesus' point is this: if an unjust judge will help the persistent widow, how much more will your Father in heaven grant your requests for your good? If He doesn't answer right away, keep praying and do not lose heart. He will answer in His time for your good.

i keep praying and praying, but God doesn't answer my prayer. Why?

I can't give you a definite answer, but I can suggest a couple of possibilities. He may be waiting to answer according to His wisdom, or He may have a better plan for you than you can envision.

Sometimes, quick deliverance isn't what's best for us. Sometimes, the Lord won't deliver us from something until the Last Day. In 2 Corinthians 12, St. Paul writes that he was afflicted with some sort of "thorn in the flesh," and he prayed repeatedly that God would remove it. Instead, the Lord responded, "My grace is sufficient for you, for My power is made perfect in weakness" (12:9). Weaknesses and afflictions can serve a purpose: they teach us how puny we truly are and how much we need the Lord's help. If that prevents us from getting proud and forsaking God, that's a good thing. Thus Paul concluded, "Therefore I will boast all the more gladly of my weaknesses, so that the power of Christ may rest upon me" (2 Corinthians 12:9).

You can't always be sure how God is going to answer your prayer. But you can be certain He will answer in the way that's best for you, because Jesus died for you (Romans 8:28).

250

My friend said all he has to do is pray in order to be forgiven. Is prayer a means of grace?

That's a great question, and one we need to answer carefully. If it's true that "God forgives me because I pray," then it means I earn forgiveness by my work of praying. That can't be true, because Jesus has done all the work to give me forgiveness. Therefore, the act of praying is not a means of grace.

However, how does one pray for forgiveness? Here's a sample prayer based on a promise of God: "Dear Father, You've promised that for

Jesus' sake You'll forgive my sin and cleanse me from all unrighteousness (1 John 1:9). Therefore, please forgive me." In that prayer, you've spoken God's Word. Jesus is present in that Word—with forgiveness. Therefore, you're forgiven—not because you prayed, but because Jesus faithfully forgave you by His work in His Word.

i never met my dad; and frankly, i hate him for it. So when you say God is my Father, it doesn't do much to comfort me. Can you pick a different metaphor?

251

I don't want to make light of your pain at all. When Jesus compares His Father to an earthly father, He is speaking of a father who gives his child good things (Luke 11:9–13). One of the greatest tragedies in this world is that there are fathers who hand out scorpions instead of good gifts to their kids. At the same time, though, I want to stick with the picture of God as a loving Father, because that's how He describes Himself to us. I will also keep you in my prayers, because God promises to help the fatherless (Psalm 10:17–18). Further, I'd encourage you to pray for yourself and your runaway dad—that you might be delivered from your anger (it will only hurt you) and that your dad might repent of his gross irresponsibility.

Does God hear the prayers of unbelievers?

The Old Testament prophet, Isaiah, gives the answer:

> Behold, the LORD's hand is not shortened, that it cannot save, or His ear dull, that it cannot hear; but your iniquities have made a separation between you and your God, and your sins have hidden His face from you so that He does not hear. **(Isaiah 59:1–2)**

At the beginning of this chapter, I noted that if the kid down the street stops by and asks me for stuff, I send him back to his own parents. When someone has put his faith in a false god (Isaiah 45:20), the Lord lets the idol do the helping. If the idol worshiper repents and trusts in Jesus, God delights to hear his prayers.

How can i know what to pray?

You can certainly examine your life, as well

as the lives of your friends and family, and pray about whatever troubles you. In addition, Martin Luther had some great advice in a letter he wrote to his barber: take one of the Ten Commandments or a portion of the creed, and pray about it. For example, take the Seventh Commandment, "You shall not steal." You could pray, "Dear Father, You command me not to steal or get anything in a dishonest way; and at the same time, You promise to provide me with everything I need. Forgive me for the times I want what others have, and forgive me when I'm jealous that others have more than I have. Therefore, help me to be content with what I have and use it in service to You, and help me to rejoice with my neighbor when he does well." You can pray that way with parts of the Small Catechism, the psalms, or all sorts of portions of Scripture.

253

How often should i pray?

1 Thessalonians 5:17 says, "Pray without ceasing." Clearly, you can't pray every minute of the day (and closing your eyes is not recommended while driving, skiing, or juggling chainsaws), but I'd set aside time each day—and whenever you are so moved. Remember, you have the privilege of speaking to your Father in heaven!

if God already knows what i need, then why should i pray?

Because you can—because the God of heaven and earth wants to hear you talk to Him so much that He gave His only Son on the cross, then commanded and invited you to pray. Your faith loves to cast your cares on the Lord (1 Peter 5:7); to fail to pray is to resist a good work that your faith wants to do.

Aren't thanks and praise part of prayer?

Absolutely, and all I wrote above applies. Thanks and praise to God are to be based upon what He has promised. Therefore, thank God for what He has done and what He says He will do—for the promises He has fulfilled and the promises He will fulfill.

What does it mean to praise God?

To praise God is to tell what He has done (Psalm 9:1)—and a lot of this has to do with declaring the promises He has made and kept, most of all the promise of Jesus who has died for your sins.

This is an important question, because people misunderstand praise and think it means talking about how much they love God. Think of the athlete who's interviewed after the big win, who says, "I just wanna give all praise and glory to God," and then he talks about himself for the next three minutes. Look, if I praise my sons for their report cards, I tell them the good job that they've done—not what a great parent I am. When we praise God, we talk about Him, not us.

When i pray, i think i sound really awkward. i'm worried that they sound so bad they're not worthy for God to hear. What do you think?

255

I think you're right, and it's a good thing you realize it. It's true for all of us, no matter how well we string words together; our prayers are still not good enough for God to hear. But God wants to hear our prayers so much that He helps.

> Likewise the Spirit helps us in our weakness. For we do not know what to pray for as we ought, but the Spirit Himself intercedes for us with groanings too deep for words.
> **(Romans 8:26)**

That's a great promise—and a great promise to pray about: "Dear Father, even though my prayers sound pretty rough, I pray that You would send the Holy Spirit to help me—because You promised to!" There you go, you've got God's Word that He'll hear your prayer.

Does God hear the prayers of people with strong faith more than people with weak faith?

No. He hears all the prayers of all His children. Remember, whether your faith is strong or weak at any given time, it still clings to Jesus and forgiveness. For Jesus' sake, God hears you.

256

i read a blog where a guy said, "God will only hear our prayer if we're willing to obey Him in what we ask." That sounds wrong, but why?

Because that means prayer depends on your intentions, on good works you haven't done yet. But prayer relies on God's promises, right? That's a good thing. Let's say I pray for patience. Why? Because I'm impatient. Do I want to be patient? No. Impatient people don't want to be patient, they want people to leave them alone or do things to please them. Therefore, when I pray for patience, I'm praying for something I really don't want by nature. So when I pray, I should confess my sin of impatience and my unwillingness to be patient, and ask that with forgiveness God would set me free to be more patient than I am.

Another blog said, "if we don't make time to speak to God in prayer, why do we expect Him to make time to speak to us?" How would you answer that?

257

I'd say, "Because God isn't a miserable, unreliable sinner like me. Even though I fail to pray as I should, He still keeps His promise and speaks to me in His Word. Only a lousy parent says to his kid, 'Since you didn't make time for me, I'm not going to take care of you.' God isn't a lousy Father. He's faithful, even when we're not. Now, that's not an excuse for us to be lousy kids; rather, it's more encouragement to trust in Him!"

James 1:5—8 says, "if any of you lacks wisdom, let him ask God, who gives generously to all without reproach, and

it will be given him. But let him ask in faith, with no doubting, for the one who doubts is like a wave of the sea that is driven and tossed by the wind. For that person must not suppose that he will receive anything from the Lord; he is a double-minded man, unstable in all his ways." Can you explain? it sounds like i shouldn't pray as long as i have any doubts, which means i won't be praying for a while.

Sure. The doubt James is talking about is doubt that God will hear your prayer. Let's approach it this way: why are you sure God hears your prayers? Because Jesus has taken away all of your sins, given you faith, and made you His child. He makes prayer certain.

If you doubt God hears your prayer, it's not just about prayer. It means you doubt Jesus. It means you doubt He's taken away all of your sins. It means you're worried God won't hear you because either Jesus hasn't done a good enough job, or you haven't done a good enough job to earn His ear. That's precisely the opposite of faith, which clings to Jesus and forgiveness.

You'll have doubt along the way. What do

you do? Confess it, because Jesus died for that sin too. Forgiven, you can be sure you're a child of God—and that God delights to hear your prayers.

It still astounds me. For Jesus' sake, God calls me His child and wants to hear me pray. Here at Casa Pauls, there are times when I just want my kids to be quiet. Not so the Lord—He's made a lot of promises to you for Jesus' sake, and He loves to hear you talk about them. Furthermore, He loves to keep His promises to you, because you're His beloved, forgiven child.

259

Section Seven: Faith and Miracles

260

"Now faith is the assurance of things hoped for, the conviction of things not seen" (Hebrews 11:1). It's God's Word, absolutely true. We can't see Jesus or His grace, but we trust in Him. We can't see the blessings of heaven, but we believe they're all ours for Jesus' sake. As my senior pastor said in the sermon last Sunday, this isn't a "hope-so" faith, but a "know-so" faith. For Jesus' sake, we know God will keep His promises.

So faith is trusting in what you do not see.

Let's add some more truth to this statement. Faith is trusting in what you do not see—often in spite of what you do see.

This is important, because there will be times when you want God to chuck His will and follow your plan. There will be times when you want to demand a miracle on your terms.

Two Lessons Learned

While writing this book, I've spent quite a bit of time at the hospital, visiting one patient over and over. Sarah is a six-year-old girl from our congregation who was diagnosed with a rare form of cancer about seven months ago. During the hideously extensive rounds of chemo and radiation therapy, she developed an equally-rare liver disease. Her body has been abused by both the illnesses and the treatments, and she's very weak. She's endured more procedures, shots, surgeries, and tubes than a lot of us will in a lifetime. Sometimes I call her "the bravest girl in the whole wide world." As I write, she's spent close to two months in the Pediatric Intensive Care Unit. She's just been moved from PICU back to Pediatric Oncology. She's far from over the liver problems, but she's gotten better. And what's her reward for getting better? More chemotherapy. That's about as fun as pulling straight A's and getting whacked with a baseball bat for your trouble.

With Sarah, there are a lot of "ifs." There's no guarantee that Sarah's going to recover. This brings me to the first reason I'm telling you about Sarah. This is a time when it's not easy to pray, "Thy will be done." I'd much rather have an instant miracle and see Sarah skip out of the hospital, but so far the Lord has other plans.

The other reason I'm telling you about Sarah is because of two important lessons I've been taught. I knew them already, but I'm always thankful when the Lord reinforces these things **262** to knuckleheads like me.

Lesson One:
The Sniffling Surgeon

The first lesson came from a doctor. Early on, Sarah had surgery to remove the cancer they'd found. A few days later, she underwent a second surgery to remove lymph nodes from various parts of her body to see if the cancer had spread. I sat with her parents during the surgery, and I was conscious of a deep divide inside me. On the one hand, I knew what was true and sure. Sarah is God's beloved child, because Jesus died for her and made her His own in Holy Baptism. Whatever the news from the operation, she had eternal life. On the other hand, I really, really wished I could tell her parents that it was all going to be okay right now, that she'd be healthy again soon. I didn't, of course, because that would be a false assurance that could only damage their faith. But I wanted to be able to. That's a big temptation whenever you face big trouble. The devil delights to make the Gospel look weak and powerless in the face of danger.

Anyway, I was present when the surgeon came out to give the results. He was sniffling, which I didn't appreciate. If a doctor is working on me, I don't want him to sound like he's got a cold. He told Sarah's parents the surgery had been successful, and the lymph nodes looked mostly cancer-free—but some looked suspicious. He gave a long account of possibilities that didn't leave us feeling very good. Then he started to cry—his sniffles were tears held back, not a cold. It's the only time I've seen a doctor cry.

Then he said the most amazing thing. He said something like, "Look, I'm a Christian. I believe that I'm God's instrument to help people in this world, and I'll do my best to help your daughter. I also believe Jesus died for Sarah. I don't know what His plans are for her, whether she'll beat this or not. But I know she belongs to Him."

Now, that was a statement of faith! Whether we saw a sudden miracle or a gradual recovery or neither, Sarah was still the Lord's. This is faith: trusting in what we do not see. Now that the doctor had stolen my devotion, I could only add my *Amen* to his words and say a prayer with the family.

Sometimes, God's promises do look really weak and useless in this world. But the Lord is faithful and He always keeps His promises.

Remember, faith is trusting in what you do not see, often in spite of what you do. If you read the previous section, Faith and Prayer, you already know the relationship between faith and miracles. Faith clings to Jesus and the forgiveness of sins. Because of that faith, all of God's promises in Christ are for you. That includes miracles like healing, deliverance from trouble, and more.

God does promise these miracles for you; however, He doesn't give a timeline. Your Father in heaven knows what's best for you— and it may be best for you to bear the cross in trouble for a while. Remember, faith prays, "Thy will be done." It knows that God has already given His Son on the cross for you, so

264

He's not going to abandon you now. Jesus shed His blood for you. Having spent that much to make you His own, God's going to keep His promises in the way that's best for you.

Lesson Two: The Bravest Girl in the Whole Wide World

I learned my other lesson from Sarah herself. When I visit her, my ongoing theme is to remind her that Jesus died for her, that God is with her, that He always keeps His promises, and He never stops looking after her. After several visits and devotions along those lines, she rolled her eyes and said with a smile in playful disgust, "Pastor Pauls, I already know that!"

265

I smiled back and said, "I know you do, Sarah. But it's my job to tell you again and again."

The lesson here is about childlike faith. We hear this in the Gospel of Mark:

> And they were bringing children to Him that He might touch them, and the disciples rebuked them. But when Jesus saw it, He was indignant and said to them, "Let the children come to Me; do not hinder them, for to such belongs the kingdom of God. Truly, I say to you, whoever does not receive the kingdom of God like a child shall

> not enter it." And He took them in
> His arms and blessed them, laying His
> hands on them. **(Mark 10:13–16)**

Jesus declares that we need to have faith like little children—in fact, the word means really little children, even infants. When you give a baby a bottle, he doesn't stop and think, "Does the giant person holding the bottle exist? Is this really for me? Have I been good enough to earn the milk?" The baby simply takes what's given. Little kids are like that with faith; we grown-ups are the ones who keep saying and thinking, "Okay, God said so, but does He really mean it?"

266

In fact, look what happens next in Mark 10:

> And as He [Jesus] was setting out on
> His journey, a man ran up and knelt
> before Him and asked Him, "Good
> Teacher, what must I do to inherit
> eternal life?" And Jesus said to him,
> "Why do you call Me good? No one is
> good except God alone. You know the
> commandments: 'Do not murder, Do
> not commit adultery, Do not steal, Do
> not bear false witness, Do not defraud,
> Honor your father and mother.'" And
> he said to Him, "Teacher, all these I
> have kept from my youth." And Jesus,
> looking at him, loved him, and said to
> him, "You lack one thing: go, sell all

that you have and give to the poor,
and you will have treasure in heaven;
and come, follow Me." Disheartened
by the saying, he went away sor-
rowful, for he had great possessions.
(Mark 10:17–22)

Right after Jesus talks about childlike faith that says, "I simply believe God gives me grace," a man runs up and says to Jesus, "What must I do to inherit eternal life?" The guy's smart enough to have riches, but he doesn't have faith. Instead of believing, "Jesus has eternal life to give to me," he's saying, "How can I earn it? What's the cost?"

Well, since the guy's asking how he can earn **267** eternal life, Jesus is going to tell him. He starts listing the Ten Commandments. After all, if you can keep all of God's Law perfectly, you're sinless! If you're sinless, you don't need forgiveness because you're already righteous in God's sight. The problem, of course, is that you can't keep God's Law. Neither can the rich man. But he thinks he can! He smugly tells Jesus he's been keeping the commandments since his youth. In response—because He loves the man—Jesus adds one more command: "Go, sell all that you have and give to the poor, and you will have treasure in heaven; and come, follow Me" (Mark 10:21).

Now, this is very, very important. Jesus is not saying, "If you're poor, you'll get to heaven." As the all-knowing Son of God, He's saying, "You've turned your riches into your god. The First Commandment says, 'You shall have no other gods before Me,' and you haven't been keeping that one. You need to get rid of your money-god and follow Me. The fact that you don't want to when I say so proves you value it more than Me. Your gold can pay for a nice funeral, but it can't raise you from the dead. I can, because I'm going to the cross to destroy the power of death."

Jesus is offering the man eternal life. He's offering him forgiveness. He's giving him faith! But the grown-up rich man doesn't want that. He walks away when Jesus proves he can't save himself. He doesn't want that childlike faith that says, "Jesus saved me and knows what's best for me."

If you're old enough to read this book, beware. It means you're old enough to think up all sorts of reasons why forgiveness isn't free or God isn't going to help you. This doesn't mean you're smart or that you're no longer naive like a child. It means you're suffering doubts about the faith God has given you. We grown-ups need to confess our constant desire to outsmart childlike faith. Like Sarah, we need to keep on confessing the Gospel we already know.

Sarah's not stupid. She's a smart six-year-old trapped in a scary, very-adult world of the PICU. She asks a lot of tough questions about tubes, needles, and liver function. But when it comes to God's promises, she knows. By God's grace, she believes. And what she believes comes out of her mouth. She's also a sinner in need of grace as much as anyone, and she can be as much of a pest in need of forgiveness as any six-year-old. But she's a baptized child of God, and she takes it on faith that she's forgiven for all of her sins.

So when I visit her, I try to use different Bible stories and verses and examples, but **269** we always come back to the same news she already knows: Jesus died for her, and He's not going to forsake her no matter what. I come back to that for a reason: that's the Gospel that strengthens her faith, that keeps her knowing what she already knows.

Miracles and Faith

Faith doesn't demand miracles on the spot. Faith also doesn't cause miracles to happen. In other words, the Lord doesn't perform miracles because people believe in Him enough. Still, a lot of people believe that faith compels God to perform miracles, perhaps for a couple of reasons. For one, it's kind of appealing to think we can force God to act by something we do, and if you already believe God saves you because you desire to be saved, why wouldn't He perform miracles for the same reason? For another, people can get this idea if they misunderstand what's going on in a lot of miracle accounts in the Bible.

There is definitely a relationship between miracles and faith in the Bible; Jesus connects the two a lot. Look at these examples.

* In Matthew 9:27–29, Jesus asks two blind men if they believe He can heal them. When they say yes, He says, "According to your faith be it done to you."

* In Mark 5, Jesus is approached by a woman who's been sick for twelve years. He says to her, "Daughter, your faith has made you well; go in peace, and be healed of your disease" (Mark 5:34).

* On the other hand, in Mark 6 we hear, "And He could do no mighty work there, except that He laid His hands on a few sick people and healed them. And He marveled because of their unbelief. And He went about among the villages teaching" (Mark 6:5–6). It sounds as if their lack of faith kept Jesus from performing miracles.

* In Mark 9, a man asks Jesus to heal his son, saying, "If You can do anything, have compassion on us and help us" (Mark 9:22). Jesus responds, "'If You can'! All things are possible for one who believes" (Mark 9:23).

* And don't forget the Canaanite woman in Matthew 15. When Jesus healed her daughter, He said, "O woman, great is your faith! Be it done for you as you desire" (Matthew 15:28).

* In Matthew 14, Jesus walks on water to calm a storm that's about to drown the disciples. Peter tries to walk on water at Jesus' command. When he fails, Jesus says, "O you of little faith, why did you doubt?" (Matthew 14:31)

271

It's no surprise people get the idea that our faith compels Jesus to help us. But this is not what Jesus is saying when He connects miracles and faith. For one thing, think back to the section where we talked about salvation. Salvation is a free gift, right? And a gift is never forced on anyone. That's why many who hear the Gospel don't believe. It's not that Jesus doesn't want them or doesn't offer enough grace. It's that they don't want the gift He's offering. They want a different god instead.

Let's look at it in a short skit that will never make it to the big screen. Here are two conversations based on Jeremiah 2:28.

First . . .

God: I've given My Son to die for you, and so I call you My child.

Believer: That's great! I believe Jesus died to take away my sins! For His sake, I belong to You!

God: Furthermore, because you belong to Me, I'm going to give you every blessing: life, salvation, daily bread, healing—everything, for Jesus' sake.

Believer: As Your child, I want those things—and I know You'll give them to me according to Your will because Jesus died for me! Thank You!

God: You're welcome. Here they come.

And . . .

God: I've given My Son to die for you, and so I call you My child.

Unbeliever: I don't want that forgiveness. I want to follow that fake, dead idol over there.

God: That's your doing, and I won't force you to live. But for Jesus' sake, I want to give you every blessing: salvation, daily bread, healing, everything.

Unbeliever: Look, I don't want Jesus.

you ask about . . . FAITH

> I don't want forgiveness. I don't want
> You or Your help. I'll take the daily
> bread, because I can snatch that away
> without believing You even exist. I'll
> let my own fake, dead idols take care
> of me, thank You.
>
> **God:** Again, I'm not going to force
> you to be forgiven. But since you
> don't want Me or My help, then I'll
> abide by your wishes. I'll let your false
> god supply your needs.

My point is this: the one who believes in Jesus can and should expect God's help. The one who doesn't believe in Jesus should not—because by rejecting Jesus, he's already said he doesn't want God's help!

273

Keep this in mind as we take a second look at the miracles above. You'll find that faith always prays, "Thy will be done," knowing God will keep His promises as He sees best.

* Jesus tells the two blind men in Matthew 9:29, "According to your faith be it done to you." What do they believe? They've already said that Jesus is the "Son of David"—the Messiah—in verse 27, and "Lord" in verse 28. They've called out, "Have mercy on us" (9:27); that's their prayer. Now, has God promised to be merciful? Yes! In fact, He's promised that the Messiah would be able to make the blind see (Isaiah 35:5). So when Jesus says to them, "Do you believe that I am able to do this?"

(Matthew 9:28), He's asking, "Do you believe that I'm the Savior, and that I keep My promises?" They say, "Yes, Lord!" They believe He can and will heal them according to His will. Therefore, Jesus says, "According to your faith be it done to you" (9:29). In other words, He says, "According to what you believe, I'm the Savior who makes the blind see. You're right! That's who I AM. By faith, you believe the faith and cling to Me. Since you desire My help by faith, I'm going to act according to My will and heal you." Do you see? Jesus doesn't heal them because they've worked hard to believe—He's healed them because He promised to, and by faith they want the gift of healing He offers.

* In Mark 5, Jesus encounters the woman who's been sick for twelve years and says, "Daughter, your faith has made you well" (5:34). Does this mean she earned the miracle by believing? No! If you start back at verse 24, you find out that she's spent all her money on doctors and is still sick. This disease is beyond human ability to cure. She's also heard reports about Jesus—in other words, she's heard the Word. The Word has given her faith—if she didn't believe, why would a sick woman drag herself through the streets to touch Him? She tells Jesus "the whole truth" that she's been incurably sick, that she's heard about Him and believes He is the Savior who can heal her . . . is this a confession of faith in the faith or what? That's when Jesus says, "Your faith has made you well." In other words, "Daughter, you heard My faith-giving Word and you believed it.

you ask about . . . FAiTH

By faith, you desire what I give, including healing.
And because I'm Me, I delight to give it to you!"
Did Jesus heal the woman because she earned
it by faith? No. He healed her because her faith
clung to the faith; it clung to Jesus and trusted
in His promises. It wasn't her doing—it was His
mercy that was responsible for the miracle.

* In Mark 6, Jesus "could do no mighty work" (6:5)
  in His hometown except for a few healings, and
  He "marveled because of their unbelief" (6:6). It
  sounds like their lack of faith made Him nearly
  powerless. That can't be, though—Jesus doesn't
  need us to believe in Him to be powerful. (If that's
  true, God couldn't have created all things without
  us around to cheer Him on!) So what was going
  on? Jesus had come to His hometown to proclaim
  that He was the Savior—and they didn't believe
  Him. They said, "It's just Mary's kid—not the Son
  of God" (see Mark 6:3)." Because they didn't
  believe He was the Savior, they didn't want Him
  to be their Savior. And because they didn't believe
  He was the Savior, they didn't want His help; they
  didn't believe He could help them. That's why He
  could only perform a few miracles—because only a
  few people desired His help!

275

* In Mark 9, the father said to Jesus, "If You can do
  anything [to heal my son], have compassion on us
  and help us" (Mark 9:22). The guy was upset and
  wavering: "I believe You're the Savior—after all,
  I'm here before You with my son, but I'm afraid
  that this evil spirit is too powerful for You. He's
  sure beaten me to a pulp." Jesus responds: "'If You

can'! All things are possible for one who believes"
(9:23). He's not challenging the man; He's cor-
recting the man's bad doctrine. He's saying, "I'm
the Savior. I'm God's Son. I have power over evil
spirits, as you've probably heard as My Word
has spread. If you believe I'm the Savior, then
know that I have the power to heal your son—all
things are possible." That's when the man says, "I
believe; help my unbelief" (9:24)! I love that! In
five words the guy says, "I believe in You, and yet
I'm a crummy sinner who still doubts Your promises. But You've promised to help me there, too,
so keep giving me faith to believe!" Jesus keeps His
promises: He heals the boy and strengthens the
dad's faith.

276

* It's the same with the Canaanite woman in
Matthew 15, whom we looked at earlier. Jesus
teaches the woman with His faith-giving Word.
By that Word, He moves her from saying, "Jesus
will help me if I can make Him like me enough" to
"Jesus will help a poor sinner like me because He's
promised to." Once He's got her faith right—once
He's got her believing His Word, He declares, "O
woman, great is your faith! Be it done for you as
you desire" (15:28). In other words, "Now you
believe My Word and My promises! Since you
want what I promise, here it is." Was it the woman's faith that compelled Jesus to heal her daughter? No! Jesus gave the gift of faith to the woman
and the gift of healing to her daughter.

* Finally, we had the example of Peter walking on
water in Matthew 14. The disciples have been

in a storm-tossed boat for several hours—they're terrified by the storm. Jesus appears to them and tells them, "Take heart; it is I. Do not be afraid" (Matthew 14:27). In other words, "Do not be afraid, because I am with you and I'm more powerful than this storm." Peter asks to walk on water with Jesus. Jesus speaks His Word to give Peter the power to do so. Peter's not walking on water because he believes hard enough, but because Jesus has spoken His Word (that causes things to happen) and Peter believes His Word. But Peter gets scared of the waves; in fact, he's more convinced of their power than Jesus'. He fears them more than he trusts Jesus' Word—the storm is becoming his god. If he's going to trust the storm's ability to kill him more than Jesus' promise to save him (thus Jesus says he has "little faith"), then the storm's going to take care of him. **277** But Jesus is merciful and saves Peter—certainly not because Peter believed enough, but because Jesus is the Savior.

You get the idea. People never forced Jesus to do miracles—how could they? He's the Son of God, not some circus performer in chains. In fact, when faithless Herod wanted to see Jesus perform some sign, he got nothing (see Luke 23:8–9). Jesus worked those miracles because He desired to and because it was a promised part of being the Messiah. The faith of people didn't compel Him to do anything; rather, their faith said, "Thy will be done," and it was His will to heal them.

Should You Expect Miracles Today?

During Jesus' public ministry on the way to the cross, He performed a lot of miracles. After His resurrection and ascension, the apostles were able to perform miracles in His name (Acts 5:12–16). Does God still work miracles today?

That answer is pretty simple: of course! He's God, and He can do whatever He wants. So maybe the better question is, "Should you expect God to work miracles today?" There are a few facets of this we need to explore.

For one thing, why were there so many miracles in the Gospels and Acts, as compared to now? Wherever Jesus went, He was healing people and working wonders. Likewise, the apostles performed a lot of miracles as the Church began. Today, we don't hear about a lot—well, except on Sunday early-morning television, where a guy is healing lots of people and would like you to send him large wads of your money, which is kind of funny because you'd think that a guy who can heal lots of people could also work some wonders on the financial end without tapping into you. Anyway, the question remains: why are there so few miracles now compared to the New Testament?

278

I've heard a few answers. Some of them are dead wrong.

For instance, some would say God doesn't work miracles today because people just don't have enough faith anymore. The Church has wandered so far away from the faith of the early Christians that today's believers just don't have enough faith to get God to act anymore. Now, I'm not going to dispute that a lot of Christianity is really messed up these days, and that a lot of those who call themselves "Christian" are only fooling themselves. (You cannot, for instance, say you are a Christian but deny that Jesus is the Christ, the eternal Son of God; or say that He now approves of **279** immorality; or say that all religions lead to heaven. God grant us a new reformation to call many to the true faith . . . but new reformation or not, He will save all of His people—He's promised!) However, we've already established that faith doesn't make God do anything. God doesn't need us to work wonders—He can do whatever He wants. Besides, is it true that all have departed from the faith of those early Christians? No! As long as we cling to the same Word they believed, we share the same faith in Christ.

Another bad explanation for the rarity of miracles today is that Jesus isn't around right now. When He was on earth, He worked miracles. Now that He's in heaven, the miracles are few and far between. This explanation overlooks a key part of the Christian faith: Jesus isn't far away. He's still present with us now. Remember what we talked about in section 5, Faith and Worship? Jesus is present with you in His Word and His Sacraments. You can't see Him, but He's there. He's not far away, pulling for you from the bleachers and hoping you stick with the faith. He visits you in His means of grace.

This leads us to the first part of the right explanation: God ordinarily works through means, not miracles. For instance, it's true that the Lord miraculously fed five thousand people (see John 6:5–14) with five loaves of bread and two fish; and it's true that He sent manna from heaven to His people for forty years in the wilderness (see Exodus 16:35). However, God normally uses means to give us daily bread. He provides farmers who grow and harvest grain, as well as bakers who make it, and grocers who sell it. Make no mistake: that's how God has ordered things to work. Likewise, Jesus healed all sorts of diseases miraculously by speaking; but normally, He provides doctors and nurses, medicines and surgeries to provide healing. That's part of His design.

This is important. Sometimes, we get the idea the world is just doing what the world does: farmers farm, bakers bake, doctors doctor, and this has nothing to do with God's plan. But they're all part of God's plan! When God created Adam, He put him in the Garden of Eden "to work it and keep it" (Genesis 2:15). Do you see? God didn't set up the whole world so everything got done directly by Him through miracles! God set up—He ordered—the world so He would use people to get much of His work done. As I said, this is huge! See, some Christians mope saying, "My life is so ordinary. God's not doing anything special for me. I wonder if I have faith." You can answer, "Life is almost always ordinary because that's how God ordered it to be. Why should you expect God to set up creation one way, then always act another? Give thanks that He provides you with what you need through the people around you. They are His instruments. God is using them for you."

281

God ordinarily works through means—but He can still work extraordinary miracles if He wants. So why were miracles frequent in the Gospels, compared to today?

Here's why: Jesus performed miracles to prove He was the Savior. The Old Testament is full of prophecies about the Messiah, so God's people would know whom to look for. In a way, those prophecies were like a checklist. For instance, Isaiah 35:5–6 declared that the Savior would make the blind see, the deaf hear, the mute sing, and the lame leap. To prove He was the Savior, Jesus healed the blind (Matthew 9:27–30), the deaf and mute (Mark 7:32–37), and the lame (John 5:2–8). When people saw Jesus do these things, they could look at the checklist of prophecies and say, "He's doing what the Bible said the Savior would do!"

In other words, Jesus performed miracles to establish His credentials.

Now, once He's established His credentials, He doesn't have to do it again. You and I don't need Jesus to perform a bunch of extraordinary wonders on us in order to prove He's the Savior. Why? Because we have His Word on it. His true Word declares that He has done these things, and our faith clings to Him and says, "Yes! Amen!" If we demand that Jesus must work miracles to prove He's the Savior, one can imagine God saying, "I've given you My Word—why is that not enough for you?"

That was the main reason for all the miracles in the Gospels. The Old Testament declared that the Savior would do these things, and Jesus did them to prove He was the Savior. Can He still perform miracles today? Absolutely! Does

He have to? No! He's already proven He's the One.

I leave you with two more things to ponder.

There's another, secondary reason why Jesus performed all those miracles: it was to give you a foretaste of heaven. Revelation 21:4 says of heaven, "[God] will wipe away every tear from their eyes, and death shall be no more, neither shall there be mourning, nor crying, nor pain anymore, for the former things have passed away." In this life, we suffer. We pray for deliverance. Sometimes the Lord provides it right away, or later, or not in this lifetime. But at the resurrection of the dead, you and I have the hope that we will be healed and delivered **283** from all affliction. Jesus showed He can do it by performing miracles. He promises He will do it on the Last Day.

Finally, the Lord works a great miracle upon you, though it's hidden beneath simple means. He's taken you—Deadguy—and made you alive forever in Him. Doctors can provide temporary healing of many diseases, at least for a while; but no one could remove one bit of your sin and guilt, except Jesus Himself. In Holy Baptism, He's already given you eternal life. In His Holy Word and Supper, He forgives you and strengthens the faith He's given. Because He gives you the grace He won on the cross, you're going to live forever.

And that, says God (Galatians 3:5), is a miracle.

Any questions?

Q&A:
You Ask . .

i can't walk, and i feel useless. Why won't God heal me so i can be an instrument for Him?

I don't know why the Lord permits you to suffer now. But I do know this: you're God's instrument right now. Sometimes He uses us as His active instruments to care for other people; and sometimes He uses us as His passive instruments—to teach others how to care. I've visited people for months who were terribly debilitated, bedridden, and unable to speak. If nothing else, they've been a testimony that life is a gift of God in a world that sees it as something to be unplugged when the going gets tough. I have no doubt they didn't want to live that way, but they endured with the hope that God would raise them fully healed for eternity.

At present, you may be largely a passive instrument—but you are one whom Jesus has redeemed, and you're one whom He uses according to His will right now. You're also one who will "leap like a deer" (Isaiah 35:6)—on the Last Day, if not before.

286 My friend's brother died. He was a Christian. We prayed for a miracle, but it didn't happen. People talk about all the good times he won't have. Why did God deprive him of a good life?

It is always an especially painful grief when somebody young dies, and talk often centers on all the good times that have been lost. This is kind thinking, but it is not sure thinking. I don't mean to sound callous, but how do we know that someone who dies young would have had a good life? What if he would have faced one setback and tragedy after another? We simply don't know what would have happened, because it didn't happen; but a "good life" isn't guaranteed in a dying world.

Your friend's family will grieve the loss of a brother and son, and I'm glad you can be an instrument of comfort for your friend. Nothing can take away that grief. But as St. Paul writes, we have hope in the midst of grief (1 Thessalonians 4:13). We don't know what kind of life this young man would have had, but we do know what kind of life he has now in Christ. For Jesus' sake, he lives forever, and he's never going to die again.

My dad is depressed. He says that if he just prays enough and trusts enough, God will heal him. What do you think?

287

I can't diagnose your dad from here, but I will offer this: if your dad had pneumonia, he'd probably go to the doctor and get some medicine. Why? Because God works through means, remember? He doesn't normally zap us with healing from out of nowhere; He uses doctors and medicine to help us get better. Mental health is no different. God provides therapists (choose carefully) and medicine to help us get better too.

So when your dad prays for healing without

using these means, he's praying for a miracle. God might grant one—but if this is a severe, clinical depression, I'd advise your dad to make use of God's gifts of trained professionals.

As long as Peter trusted in Jesus, he could walk on water. Does that mean as long as i trust in Jesus, i can walk on water too?

No, because Jesus didn't tell you to. That was just for Peter. Jesus has much better stuff to speak to you anyway such as, "I forgive you."

288

You said Jesus performed miracles in order to prove His authority. Why did the apostles perform miracles?

The apostles performed miracles to demonstrate that they were Jesus' spokesmen. Jesus gave them the authority to do miracles in His name.

Does my pastor need to perform miracles to prove that he speaks Jesus' Word?

Well, there are a couple of ways to answer this. On the one hand, every time a pastor speaks the Gospel, sins are forgiven and people are made righteous before God. Every time he performs a Baptism, the one baptized is raised to life. Get the idea? Of course, it's not the pastor performing the miracles; it's the Lord at work in His Word.

But you probably mean to ask, "Does my pastor need to perform wonders like healing the sick to prove that he speaks Jesus' Word?" As cool as that would be, the answer is no. You don't measure a pastor's faithfulness by the miracles he performs. You measure it by whether his preaching is faithful to God's **289** Word. Remember, Jesus already proved His authority—and the authority of His Word—by the miracles He worked. He doesn't have to prove His authority again.

On Pentecost (in Acts 2), the Lord worked wonders like tongues of fire and the sound of a loud rushing wind before the disciples spoke in different languages. How come He doesn't do stuff like that at church anymore?

God did provide those signs on Pentecost,

the birthday of His New Testament Church. If you like, you can think of those wonders as the fireworks display to celebrate. But don't forget what else happened that day: three thousand people believed the Gospel, were baptized, and went on to devote themselves to the Word, to receive Holy Communion, and to pray (Acts 2:41–42).

When we gather in worship, we don't have the tongues of fire or sound of wind. But then again, God never promised that He forgives sins with such things. We do have the gifts of His Word, Holy Baptism, and Holy Communion. In other words, we have His means of grace, by which He gives forgiveness, faith, and eternal life—and that's a far greater miracle!

290

You talked about "Lord, have mercy" in a previous chapter, and how that's in the liturgy. That's what people cried out to Jesus in a lot of miracle accounts in the Bible. Is there a connection?

Very good! People cried out, "Lord, have mercy" because (a) they believed Jesus was the Lord, (b) they believed He would have mercy, and (c) He was there. He was present with them. When Jesus was walking around Jerusalem, people weren't standing on empty streets in Nazareth yelling, "Lord, have mercy!" at empty air.

That's why it's a great prayer as part of the liturgy—because it declares that the Lord Jesus is present with us in His Word and His Sacraments. That's why it's a great prayer for you too. When you were baptized, Jesus promised you, "I am with you always, to the end of the age" (Matthew 28:20).

Can the devil work wonders?

He can. Back in Exodus, Pharaoh's magicians did some pretty weird stuff by their "secret arts" (see Exodus 7:22, 7:11, and 8:7). The origin of their power certainly wasn't God. The devil also can afflict people with disease (Luke 13:16). Furthermore, there is nothing in Scripture that would prevent Satan from healing someone, if that served his purposes.

291

Why would the devil heal anybody?

The devil likes to appear as "an angel of light" (2 Corinthians 11:14). After all, if he presented himself as a stinky demon out to destroy, he wouldn't be quite so attractive. It wouldn't be beyond possibility for the devil to work some miracle of healing—if he could use that to distract you from salvation. If he can get you so distracted by some wonder that you forget all about your need for forgiveness, he'd be more than happy to give you health for a while. Think of it this way: if there were a church where everybody was healed of their sicknesses for a while, but none were forgiven, they'd all be healthily headed for hell.

Can miracles lead people astray?

Yes, if people focus on the miracle rather than on Jesus' grace. Faith clings to forgiveness, not wonders. If someone clings to wonders instead, then he doesn't have faith. A prime example is John 6:15. Jesus has just fed five thousand men with five loaves of bread and two fish—truly a miracle. He's done this to prove He's the Savior of all those Old Testament prophecies, right? He's done this to prove He's the One whom the Old Testament said would die for the sins of the world (Isaiah 53:3–5), right?

What do the people do? They try to make Jesus a king who will just give them bread for the rest of their lives! They're so distracted by the miracle, they just want a free lunch until they die. But if all they get from Jesus is bread—but not forgiveness—they're going to die forever. That's what happens when people focus on signs and wonders, not on the grace Jesus won on the cross. But the cross is the greatest miracle of all.

God can still work miracles; and when He does, we give thanks. But He has better plans for you than temporary wonders in this world. He's given His Son to die for you, so you can live forever. That's what faith clings to.

So how can i be certain that a miracle or wonder is God's doing, and not Satan's?

293

Just keep your eyes focused on the cross. Rejoice that the Lord has given you faith, and by faith cling to Jesus and the forgiveness He gives. He's conquered the devil, and the devil can only do what the Lord permits. If—and I think it's a big if—the devil were to heal you of some disease, you'd never know. Instead, you'd give thanks to Jesus for the healing. Would *that* ruin the devil's day or what?

What do you think of "faith healers"?

I'm extremely skeptical. I've had contact

with very few, but the message has always been, "If you believe enough, God will heal you." That's the same argument as, "If you believe enough, God will answer your prayer." Here are a couple of things to remember.

Let's say it was true that as long as you have enough faith, God will heal you. That would mean you're healthy as long as you have faith, right? Logically, it would also mean that if you got sick, you didn't have enough faith; and if you were dying, your faith must be really weak or gone. And it would mean everyone who dies just doesn't have enough faith anymore. No one would be getting to heaven.

The other thing is this: remember that faith never makes demands on God, but prays, "Thy will be done." When Jesus healed the woman in Mark 5, she'd been sick for twelve years. I'm sure this wasn't the first time she'd wanted to be healed. Sometimes, the Lord permits suffering in our lives to teach us (Hebrews 12:6); to be our strength and show us our need for His grace (2 Corinthians 12:9); to demonstrate that He saves by faith in Jesus—not human wisdom or strength (1 Corinthians 1:27–29); or for some other reason.

The God who saves you is all-powerful and works wonders. That's a great comfort for you and me. At the same time, He chooses to save us in what appears to be the weakest and most shameful of plans. He becomes flesh and dies on the cross to take away our sins. It's Jesus' death in your place that saves you.

Therefore, it's completely consistent with God's will that we live lives that don't have a whole lot of signs, wonders, and miracles attached to them. God doesn't save by wonders. He saves you by His Son. Often for us, the miracles of healing and deliverance we desire are reserved for the Last Day, when we're raised from the dead. In the meantime, though, Jesus is faithful. He still visits us in His Word and Sacraments, forgiving our sins and strengthening our faith.

295

The prophet Habakkuk lived in a time where his nation had forsaken God, where he witnessed sin and treachery all around him. There wasn't much good or wonderful to see, but what did the Lord declare? "The righteous shall live by his faith" (Habakkuk 2:4). That's true for you and me too. When God provides miracles for us, thanks be to God! Even when He doesn't, He's already given us forgiveness. He's already given us faith. By faith, we cling to Jesus—and we know that, in His time, deliverance will come.

I've just returned from a quick visit with
Sarah. She turned seven on Saturday and got
her feeding tube removed, so I brought her a
birthday donut. I told her to feed it twice a day
and make sure it got enough sleep. She said I
was goofy and that she'd eat it as soon as she
finished physical therapy. It's good to see her
smile. Her parents have reminded me that
Sarah's come a long way in the past few weeks,
and that the ICU nurses call her the "miracle
girl." Indeed, amid all the standard procedures
of treatment, the Lord has worked some amazing things for Sarah's good. It's a wonder that
she's still with us—not a random stroke of luck,
but the Lord's wonderful care along the way.

The Lord, who created all things, still weaves
the days together and works all things for our
good. We understand that and see it better at
some times than others. But His love for us is
always sure, because it's all done for the sake
of Jesus.

A Parting Truth: It's All about Jesus

298

We've talked about *faith* and *the faith* for a while now, and it's time to wrap it up. So here's a parting thought that I hope is obvious by now: it's all about Jesus.

The Word is all about Jesus. The first thing God does when Adam and Eve sin is promise them Jesus is coming (Genesis 3:15). He tells them about the Savior so by His Word, they can believe in Him. Throughout Scripture, the Word proclaims Jesus. The Old Testament declares He is coming. The Gospels tell how

you ask about . . . FAITH

the Word-made-flesh (John 1:14) is born, lives, dies, rises, and ascends for you. The Epistles tell about living as His people until He returns again in glory.

The Christian faith is all about Jesus. We get the faith—the teachings of Christianity—from the Bible. As the Bible is all about Jesus, so is the Christian faith. People can believe God is powerful and holy and good. But apart from Jesus, they can't be Christians (John 14:6). All of Christian doctrine points to Jesus. The Law shows us our sin and our need for Him. The Gospel declares Him so we might believe and be forgiven.

So faith is all about Jesus too. It's His gift **299** to us so we might believe in Him. And because it's His gift by His work, we can be sure that it saves. It saves because it clings to Him and His forgiveness. Because that forgiveness is His gift by His work, it's certain too.

And because we're forgiven, our works are good and pleasing to God.

Worship is all about Jesus, because Jesus visits us in His Word and Sacraments to give us forgiveness and strengthen our faith.

Prayer is about Jesus too. God keeps His promises to us for Jesus' sake.

Among the promises God keeps are promises

of miracles—if not now, then on the Last Day. Why will God keep these promises? Because of Jesus.

It's all about Him.

Hebrews 11 is a fascinating chapter of the Bible: it's a catalog of believers who lived by faith. Trusting in the promises of God, they obeyed His Word even though they couldn't see the reason or benefit with their eyes. At the start of Hebrews 12, we're instructed to fix our eyes on "Jesus, the founder and perfecter of our faith, who for the joy that was set before Him endured the cross, despising the shame, and is seated at the right hand of the throne of God" (12:2).

That's faith: clinging to Jesus who has redeemed us at the cross. Whatever life holds for you, Jesus is your life and salvation. By the faith He gives you to cling to Him, all of His good gifts are yours.